**Books are to be returned on or before
the last date below.**

Pub Walks
in
The Cheshire Fringes

T

WITHDRAWN

Neil Coates

Published by Sigma Leisure – an imprint of
Sigma Press, 1 South Oak Lane, Wilmslow, Cheshire SK9 6AR, England.

British Library Cataloguing in Publication Data
A CIP record for this book is available from the British Library.

ISBN: 1-85058-695-0

Typesetting and Design by: Sigma Press, Wilmslow, Cheshire.

Cover photograph: The Blacksmith's Arms, Broughton Mills

Maps and photographs: Neil Coates

Printed by: MFP Design and Print

Walks Checked by: Donna Shaw

Disclaimer: the information in this book is given in good faith and is believed to be correct at the time of publication. No responsibility is accepted by either the author or publisher for errors or omissions, or for any loss or injury howsoever caused. Only you can judge your own fitness, competence and experience.

Preface

Images of the heart of Lakeland adorn the walls of Tourism Offices the world over and stare out at you from the pages of countless guidebooks, as familiar as the view from your front window. A thousand cars an hour pour into Windermere whilst a thousand pairs of boots tramp up Cat Bells on a summer weekend, Wordsworth's crowd reborn as a host of yellow cagoules. The boat trips, the landscapes of poem and prose, the accessible highlights of England's favourite acres all ensure that the Lake District is one of the most visited National Parks in the world. But you don't have to add to the congestion so-created to experience the best of Lakeland. This book dares you to be different and explore the fringes of the National Park. You'll be in good company, too: it is said that Wordsworth's favourite places were in these fringes, little changed from his day 150 years ago. Tennyson, Coleridge and Keats, too, all favoured these less-frequented areas.

The walks featured are all just inside or outside the National Park boundary or meander in and out of the Park, offering the best of both worlds – beauty with space and tranquillity. Here, too, are lakes and tarns, mountain paths and riverside strolls, picturesque villages hidden in the folds of the hills, mellow old watermills nestling beside packhorse bridges. Here, also, are vast vistas across mountain, moor and sea, to the mountains of Scotland, the Isle of Man, Snowdonia and the backbone of England, the Pennines. The boundary of the National Park is an arbitrary line on a map; less tenuous and much more permanent is the tangible beauty of the hills, lakes, valleys and shoreline which know no such artificial limits.

The visitable past is also here in abundance, more so, indeed, than in the over-visited central areas. Stone circles and monoliths, Roman ruins and the footsteps of saints, Viking crosses and monastic sites, Norman castles and the varied heritage of the industrial era are liberally scattered in the hidden places of old Cumberland, Westmorland and Lancashire-over-the-Sands.

The only thing you won't find are crowds. These fringes retain a serenity and peace long gone from the tourist trail, the roads relatively quiet, the bridleways, footpaths and byeways refreshingly uncluttered, the commons, hills and valleys dotted with ponies and sheep rather than crocodiles of walkers.

Best of all for the discerning reader of this book, there are splendid village pubs, town taverns and country inns, many offering beers brewed by the growing number of tiny breweries to be found in Cumbria (the 1998 CAMRA Champion Bitter is brewed at one such). All of the walks either start at or near to such pubs, or pass one or more such establishments along the way, all in all an added temptation to stand out from the crowd!

The walks featured in the book are a personal choice aimed at taking you to and through as varied a selection of countryside and heritage as possible. You'll lose nothing of the grandeur of the high peaks, for the fringes of the National Park are the place where these mountains sink into the sea or surrender to the furrowed fells. Nor should the lover of watery backgrounds despair, some of the lesser visited, but equally beautiful, lakes lie in these fringes whilst smaller tarns dapple the commons and craggy fells explored on the routes. Remarkable views are two a penny, many better than those to be had from much more famous viewpoints. And you'll still need decent walking boots or shoes and suitable outdoor clothing, none of the walks are for the patent leather and pacmac brigade. Everything, indeed, is here for a decent few days out in England's favourite corner except the patience (or aggression!) needed to fight for parking spaces, a vacant spot on a crowded hill or a traffic queue to wile away the time in.

My thanks go to the various licensees, landlords/ladies and owners of the many and varied pubs and inns whom I buttonholed during the course of the original research for this book in the summer and autumn of 1998. All maintain beer, property, fittings and conversation to the highest order of excellence, many are founts of information and asides about local countryside and community history and no few are keen ramblers themselves. Go on – indulge yourselves!

Neil Coates

Contents

The Walks

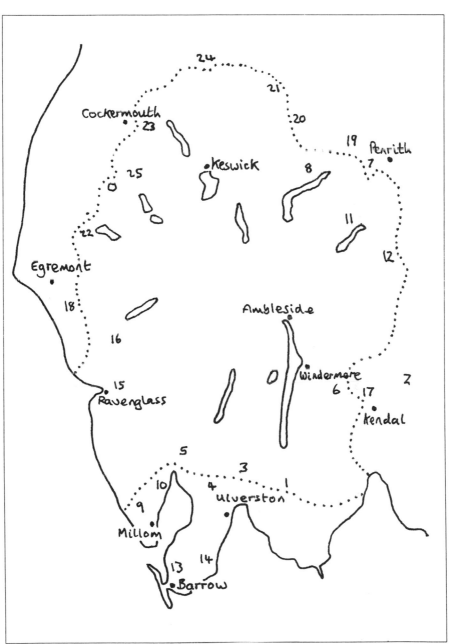

Locations of the walks

Problem-free perambulations

Out & about

None of the walks featured in this book should pose any problems to those with a modicum of fitness Most include climbs and descents of varying degrees and feature a good mix of field paths, farm tracks, by-roads, miners' roads and so on – in short, the sort of variety of terrain and traction that make for a good day's walking. None reach any great height or remote areas, yet all can offer both sublime views and solitude. A few simple precautions should ensure that no problems of your own making spoil a day out in the fringes of Lakeland. Wear adequate clothing and carry a waterproof and spare warm clothing in the colder months. Carry a high energy snack (e.g. peanuts, mint cake, chocolate bars) and a drink. A decent pair of walking shoes or boots are a must – town shoes or sandals aren't really suitable to tackle wet stepping stones, loose scree, boggy pastures, upland sheep tracks or slippery field paths. It's all common sense really.

Accidents do happen, however. If you're involved in one which renders you unable to walk, then get your walking companion (or a passing rambler if you're a solo walker) to telephone 999 and ask for Mountain Rescue, passing on the details requested by the respondee (in particular an accurate fix on your location). Bear in mind, though, that this is an emergency service. They're not there to answer queries from walkers who have lost their bearings, from those wishing to get the latest weather forecast or to advise those who draw blood during an argument with a thorn tree or barbed wire. All of these, and worse, have happened, don't **you** add to these tales of folly. The Mountain Rescue Teams are totally professional yet almost entirely staffed, funded and equipped by volunteers and through charitable donation. Many pubs in Cumbria have on their bar a charity box dedicated to supporting this service – a few pounds, pence or Euros to lighten your load may one day help to save your life, so please don't studiously ignore such boxes . . . help fill them!

The Walks

Short walks and long walks, high walks and low walks – all are here included! They should not be taken lightly, most will require at least 3 hours, many of them more like a full day. It's really of no value to ascribe a time to any of these walks as each individual walker best knows his or her level of fitness and walking speed. I'd recommend that you read the relevant chapter through before commencing the walk, as within the narrative are highlighted such problems or features as may be encountered – particularly boggy sections, steep climbs, viewpoints to linger at, etc. Only then will you have an idea as to how long it may take *you* to do the walk. As a very general rule of thumb, few casual ramblers would expect to cover much more than 2 miles in an hour in such varied terrain as that included in this book.

Each walk is self-contained and includes easy to follow directions which should ensure you complete the day out without problems of navigation. The sketch maps are simply that, drawn on the hoof and intended to offer outline guidance as to progress along the walk and highlighting particular features or points of interest. The scales are only very approximate and the detail is there for information rather than accuracy. They're certainly not geographically accurate to the nearest hundred yards! Many people may wish to identify other points adjacent to a particular walk or orient themselves with more distant features. To do so, it's best to have a copy of the relevant Ordnance Survey map for the area. The new editions of the "Outdoor Leisure" sheets for The English Lakes NW, NE, SE, SW, updated to 1998, are ideal for these purposes; all of the walks included in this book are within the areas included on one or more of these maps.

All of the walks use statutory rights of way (roads, bridlepaths, public footpaths, etc.) unless otherwise stated. On a few occasions the routes stray from such definitive rights of way. These may be, for example, over land to which access has been granted in "blanket" agreements, such as National Park Access Land, land owned by North West Water (whose written policy is to allow free access unless otherwise stated at any particular site – for example to protect particularly sensitive ecological sites, nesting areas, etc.), on National Trust land which is generally open to all, on common land or to particular viewpoints and hilltops which have been used by locals and visitors for decades whilst not actually designated as within the public domain. One or two utilise concessionary paths, negotiated between the relevant local authority and the landowner. Things change over time, and it may be that such agreements are changed, cancelled or extended. The walk descriptions given in this book are given in good faith and do not, so far as the writer can ascertain, encourage trespass onto areas not outlined above.

All of the walks have some sections on roads. The vast majority of these are minor roads and back lanes with very little traffic. On occasion, however, it proves necessary to utilise short stretches of main road to make links between paths and tracks. These stretches are emphasised where appropriate in the text. Particular care should be exercised on these short stretches as the main roads in Cumbria are largely without verges. The sight-lines are generally adequate, allowing you to see vehicles well in advance, and hopefully vice-versa. Walk in single file facing oncoming traffic, make yourself visible to oncoming traffic (hold this book or a map in your left hand as a "flag"), keep dogs and children on a tight leash and, if it seems advisable, cross to the "wrong" side (i.e. the left of the road) to safely negotiate sharper right-hand bends where oncoming traffic can't see you easily.

Nature bare in tooth & claw

Feedback from earlier books suggests that domesticated stock, and in particular cattle, still cause unease and uncertainty amongst many walkers. There really is no need to feel threatened by such farm animals – there's more of a chance that you'll be hit by a meteorite or win the lottery jackpot than be harmed by animals on a countryside ramble. Nonetheless, a few pointers may be of some comfort to those of a nervous disposition. By law (in theory at least), no farmer should permit a bull to be left alone in any field which is crossed by a public right of way. Farmers can, however, leave a bull in such a field so long as it is accompanied by cows. This appears to make the bull docile and disinterested in anything but the obvious and grazing sedately. If you're deliberately provocative then that's your look-out. Just strolling normally, however, you can pass within a few yards of a grazing bull and excite no interest whatsoever.

In practice you'll not often find a bull in a field, so any cattle you'll encounter will either be young heifers, cows grazing between milkings or bullocks grazing to put on the required weight for market (no farmer would leave two bulls in the same field as they're totally incompatible). In all cases the animals may well be a little inquisitive, particularly so younger herds of bullocks, which may congregate behind you and follow in your footsteps. They're all-but harmless, turning in your tracks to face them will effectively halt them and cause some back-tracking on their part. The message is, simply, that cattle are curious but pretty timid; expect them to take notice when you pass through their home (for such it is), so just walk at normal pace, giving them a berth if they're lying across the route of the footpath and don't deliberately get between a cow and her (usually) nearby calf. The far stile or gate will soon be there!

Personally, I find horses are far more curious and liable to actually approach you than any other beastie – and they have big teeth too! Ignoring them invariably works, keep those mints and apples for your own consumption. You're very unlikely to find pigs in any field that you cross (you'll be totally lost if you find any in fields featured in this book). If you do then beware, as these are probably potentially the most dangerous and aggressive of all farm animals, especially when there are also piglets in tow. Great to look at, a disaster to linger around. If you do find pigs then find an alternative route, through a parallel field for example. More exotic animals are also now found with increasing frequency the British countryside. Llamas and Alpacas apparently tend to spit, and seem to have teeth as large as those of horses, so again find an alternative route around that particular field. Ostriches and emus – keep at least one parish between you and them. The Beast of Bodmin Moor – you've purchased the wrong book.

Finally, if you see the cloven-hoofed Bogle, with its distinctive striped coat, stiff mane, large ears, wild eyes and loping gait, then you've spent several hours too long at the bar. Forget the walk, for you're sure to encounter Goody-esque Friesian cows waiting to leap onto you from tree branches, or fearsome sheep flashing from behind trees. Sleep it off and hope for good weather and no hangover the following day!

Pubs, pints and parking

Opening times

With publicans able to open their doors legally between 11am and 11pm (on Sundays 12 noon to 10.30pm), there is scope for a wide range of opening hours; the pubs and inns featured in this book take full advantage of such legislative eccentricity. Wherever possible, details of opening hours are given in the pub section at the start of each chapter, such details being obtained from the licensee and/or staff when the research for the book was undertaken, the latter half of 1998. The licensed trade is, however, renowned for the rapid turnover of licensee, particularly in the case of brewery owned pubs (as opposed to free houses), and the continuity of opening hours may be equally ephemeral. In general, the pubs featured all open at least during the evenings (6/7pm-11pm) Mondays to Fridays, most also have a lunchtime session from 12 noon to 3pm. At weekends, most are open all permitted hours. Variations, however, abound – some have differing hours for summer and winter, for school holiday periods, for high days and holidays, etc. The message is, you'll be unlucky to find a particular pub closed during the hours cited in each walk introduction, but it could happen; equally, however, hours may have been extended and improved, a happy chance enough to bring a smile to the face of any discerning rambler and drinker. Cheers!

The village pub

That most British of institutions, the village pub, is increasingly an endangered species. A defining characteristic (along with the church and squire's house) of any village in times past, many now only have a tenuous hold on viability, and on your travels throughout Cumbria you'll readily identify many a former pub now put to residential use. All the country and village pubs visited in this book appear to be thriving, but don't let this make you take them for granted. The visitor who simply parks up in the handy pub car park, rambles off and then returns and leaves without dropping in to the pub is potentially another nail in the coffin of this much-loved institution. "Use them or lose them" is a suitable slogan to appropriate from other fields. Most licensees – certainly all the ones whose premises feature in this volume – are a fount of information about the local area, even if they've only been in-post for a matter of months. An hour spent in the pub in question before, during or after you've enjoyed your walk, can only add to the pleasure of your day out. It'll also help to ensure that the next generation of walkers, visitors and locals alike will be able to partake in at least this aspect of the village idyll.

Breweries and beers

In common with most other areas of England, Cumbria has seen a flowering of new, small-scale "micro" breweries over the past decade. Whilst some were destined to be short-lived, others have survived and thrived, providing a welcome extension of choice to the discerning drinker and adding variety to the few long-established breweries whose products still dominate the market regionally. The main players in Greater Lakeland are Jennings of Cockermouth, owning about 110 pubs and supplying a wide free trade, Robinson's of Stockport who took over and closed the old Hartleys Brewery in Ulverston and whose pubs (around 55) still carry the Hartleys name, and Scottish & Newcastle Breweries, selling widely throughout the area under the Theakston name. The smaller breweries are, however, the icing on the cake, and the pubs featured in this book will introduce you to several such – Yates of Westnewton, Bitter End of Cockermouth, Dent Brewery, Cartmel Brewery, Coniston Brewery, Hesket Newmarket Brewery, The Derwent Brewery, are all well worth seeking out, whilst others are in the proverbial pipeline. Such, indeed, is the quality of the locally produced beers in this area that Coniston Brewery's "Bluebird" bitter won the coveted Champion Beer of Britain title, awarded by CAMRA at the National Beer Festival in London in August 1998. Catch it if you can!

Parking at the pub

Most the walks start at a particular pub, the vast majority of which have a dedicated car park. It's accepted practice at most such pubs that walkers who arrive before opening time will leave their car in the car park and pop in for a pint upon their return. If at all possible, try to get the agreement of the licensee before you set out, particularly so at weekends and during the busier summer weeks; it's unlikely that you'll be refused. An alternative is to park up at a suitable place near to the start of the walk, for instance the village car park, near to the church, in a lay-by. Whatever you do, don't block any field gates, access roads, etc. Heed, too, the cautionary tale above, and don't leave a pub's car park without visiting; after all, you wouldn't expect someone to park in your driveway for a few hours during a football match without so much as a by-your-leave, then depart without a word of thanks or apology – the principle's the same! Treated in the right spirit, "Parking for Patrons Only" can be a very welcoming sign.

Public transport

Whilst the frequency of bus and train services in Cumbria is often very poor, there are some excellent facilities which make accessing some of the walks in this book by public transport both easy and convenient. The whole coastal strip (with the exception of the Solway Firth) retains a rail service with regular trains Mondays to Saturdays plying the scenic Cumbrian Coast line, an excellent day out in itself. In addition, the branch line from Oxenholme to Windermere offers easy access to the "Queen of the Lakes" from the Lancashire conurbations, Manchester and Manchester Airport whilst Penrith Station, on the main West Coast line between England and Scotland, is a good jumping off point for the northern area of Lakeland. In the south Ulverston, Barrow and the Furness Peninsula have a reasonable daily service to and from Lancaster, Preston and Manchester.

Bus services complement the rail lines and fill in many of the gaps. Regular daily services link most of the main towns to each other from early morning to mid evening, whilst village services often run once or twice a day. These are complemented by school buses during term times (and which can be used by anyone, not just schoolchildren) and, during the summer, a network of recreational services which open up areas not usually served by buses, including the Caldbeck and Lorton Fells and the Kentmere Valley.

Outline details of current services are given, where appropriate, in the introductory panel to each of the walks. It is important to check these details before you commence your day out to ensure that timings and/or service numbers have not altered since December 1998. The Cumbria County Journey Planner information and help line is the place to contact. The telephone number for all bus, rail and boat times is **Carlisle (01228) 606000** (staffed 9am to 5pm Mondays to Fridays, 9am to 12 noon Saturdays). Many of the Tourist Information Centres throughout Cumbria will also be able to help with enquiries; most of these are open Mondays to Saturdays throughout the year with many also open on Sundays, particularly in the main towns.

Walk 1. Bigland Tarn

Route: Haverthwaite – Roudsea Wood – Bigland Tarn – High Brow Edge

Terrain: One long, moderate climb, otherwise easy going

Distance: 6½ miles

Start: The Rusland Pool, near Haverthwaite

Map: O.S. Outdoor Leisure Sheet – "The English Lakes (SE)"

Access: The Rusland Pool Hotel stands beside the A590 some 3 miles SW of Newby Bridge. Ample parking at the Hotel or on the adjoining old A590, now a long lay-by.

Public transport: Infrequent Monday to Friday service 595, Kendal to Barrow bus service; other seasonal and weekend services. All pass the Rusland Pool.

The Rusland Pool (01229 861384)

The Saddle Bar is the featured pub for this walk, tucked away to the rear of the Rusland Pool Hotel. Seasoned visitors to Lakeland may remember this pleasant hotel as The Dickson's Arms, its name until about 1996. Handily open all day (12 noon to 11pm, 10.30pm on Sundays), it's a very comfortably appointed Bar featuring very low beamed ceilings – if you're much over 6 foot tall then beware! The walls are dotted with a mixture of country prints and old photographs, the beams and shelves with brasses, ornate vases and willow-pattern plates. As a change from the more usual floral pattern or moquette, the wall benches and scatter chairs are upholstered with a cloth depicting hunting scenes.

At one end a wood-burning stove pumps out the calories in winter, at the other you can regain calories lost during your walk by partaking of the well kept Wadworth's 6X bitter and the extensive range of bar meals, available throughout the day up to 9.15pm. The Saddle Bar is set well back from the main A590, huddled beneath a wooded hillside above the curiously named Rusland Pool River. You should be able to enjoy a pint sat outside on a terrace, but this is subject to the whims of Lake District Special Planning Board planners who are currently insisting that the terrace be demolished. The whole sorry tale is prominently outlined in newspaper cuttings and features displayed by the bar. Inside or out, The Rusland Pool is an ideal base from which to explore this under-visited end of the Furness Fells, where the wooded hills give way to the peaceful, serene levels of the Leven Estuary.

A reedy corner of Bigland Tarn

The Walk

Walk up to the main road, but turn left immediately before reaching it and walk along the tarred footpath, which runs below the carriageway level, and beside a hedge. In about 150 yards turn right up the bank and carefully cross this very busy A590. Cross the bridge over the Rusland Pool and immediately beyond it on the right is a footpath sign. Cross the stile to join the path along the top of an embankment alongside the river.

The embankment protects the low-lying pasturelands from the high tides of the Leven Estuary. Remain with it for the next mile or so, a peaceful stroll rich in wildflower interest in spring and summer, with great drifts of vetch and the distinctive purple flowers of Devil's Bit Scabious held on the end of long stems. The estuary holds rich pickings for a wide variety of wading birds, curlew and oystercatchers appear common whilst the meadows are home to the increasingly uncommon skylark and meadow pipit. Otters are known to frequent the waters hereabouts, benefiting from the sea trout for which the Leven is renowned. Further afield, the eye is drawn to the heavily wooded line of hills that stretch ahead-left away to the horizon, the Ellerside hills marking the western fringe of the Cartmel Peninsula. To the right (west) are glimpses of the Barrow Monument on The Hoad, above the old port of Ulverston. This memorial to the locally born Secretary to the Admiralty in the early years of Victoria's reign is, fittingly, in the style of a lighthouse. At some point soon after the small outflow on your right, cut down from the embankment to trace the waterside fence, eventually reaching a stile giving access to the long abandoned railway line between Ulverston Junction and Lakeside.

Cross the old bridge here and turn immediately left once over the stile at the far end of the bridge. The path winds through high bracken, emerging as a wooded riverside way. Bear right at the fork (ignoring the old footbridge down to the left) and strike through the trees to a tarred lane; turn left along this. The woodlands to your right are part of the Roudsea Wood and Mosses National Nature Reserve, to which access is restricted to permit holders. Several hundred acres are protected as prime examples of the contrasting and diverse woodland to be found on limestone and slate rock, together with rare lowland peat bogs home to uncommon insects and plants.

Stay with this un-trafficked tarred lane, signed as the route of the Cumbrian Coastal Way, for the next mile or so, passing by a fishing hut to reach a cattle grid beside the tumbled remains of a slate-built cottage. Immediately across the grid take the sign-posted footpath on the left, crossing a concrete footbridge and the kissing gate beyond. Beyond the next kissing gate bear half-right across the neck of pasture to a further gate, here rejoining the riverside path. You'll soon reach a tarred lane, turn left to its end. The way now is right, along the busy road to Cark and Grange. On reaching the junction with the narrow road coming in from the left (c. 200 yards), cross the road but don't go along the narrow road. Remain with the main road for another 100 yards to the sharp right bend where, on the left, a Coastal Way footpath sign points up into the woods.

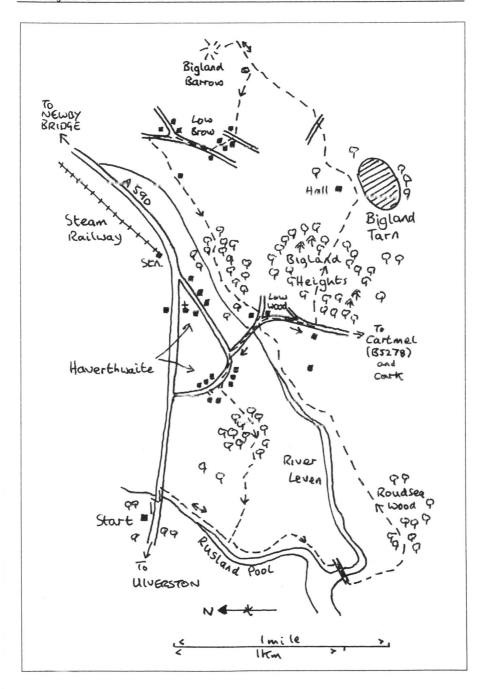

The path steepens, following what can be a veritable streambed in wet weather, and commences a steady climb up Bigland Heights. After a distance the path levels out and becomes braided, simply continue ahead through the rhododendrons, soon ascending again to a crossing of forestry roads. Go straight across, climbing the steeper, somewhat rougher roadway. Pausing for breath at the isolated waymark post, take time to lap up the views behind, now encompassing a widening panorama of southern Lakeland, with Haverthwaite nestling in woods beside the Leven in the valley far below. Continuing the climb, Bigland Beck tumbles in torrents to your left. Pass through the woodland edge gate and walk ahead, the occasional low waymark post leading to a declivity in the low ridge, beyond which the delightful Bigland Tarn is revealed, nestling below low fells and wooded slopes.

Rich in wildfowl, the dual joys of this idyllic place is its tranquillity and, in summer, the magnificent displays of water lilies which cover perhaps a quarter of the tarn. It's used as a coarse fishery, but other than the occasional angler you may, despite the growing reputation of the outdoor activities centred on the Bigland Estate, quite possibly be the only people here at this peaceful spot hidden in the hills. The way is left, through the kissing gate and along a path above the waterside. Nearby, but only glimpsed occasionally, is the magnificent country house of Bigland Hall. The path leads shortly to a crossing of tarred lanes in the estate grounds; signs hint at various leisure activities available here. You should turn right, cross the cattle grid and trace the estate drive to the gates and a minor road. Go straight across and through the gate signposted as a path to Hazelrigg.

Bear left beyond the gate, passing to the left of the security fencing surrounding gas installations. The well-trodden path winds through rough pastures coloured by harebells and foxgloves riffling in the summer breeze. Passing through the old gateway, rise gradually to find a small tarn on your left, immediately before which is a stone step stile and a 4-way signpost, rather difficult to spot in the high bracken of summer. The way is left here, but it's worth carrying on ahead a few hundred yards to take in the remarkable views.

Many people take advantage of an old observation platform built on the summit of Bigland Barrow, reached by climbing the stone step stile just to the right of a gate you'll see off to your left at a fork in the path. This, however, is not officially on a public right of way, so make your own judgement (a note of caution, the ladder up the tower is somewhat worn). The views are breathtaking, taking in the great majority of the central and southern peaks of the Lake District whilst to the east the long line of the Pennines forms a backdrop, the distinctive peak of Ingleborough taking the eye. At the foot of the Barrow is a large, well established artificial tarn blending in perfectly to its setting.

Return to the small tarn, climb the stile and pass by the water on your right. Continue ahead over the slight rise and look ahead right to the junction of stone walls just beyond the area of high (and boggy) tussock grass. By the corner here, climb the stile and pick a way half-left through the boggy area immediately beyond. In a hundred or so yards you'll be able to see a farm in the dip below, with a walled green track leading back from it towards you. Work your way down to the gate at your end of this track, and then follow it to the road by the farm. Turn right, then almost immediately left down the narrow tarred lane. Fall with this past a number of cottages here at High Brow Edge to reach another minor road, along which turn right.

At the junction bear left downhill. From here are impressive views up the gorge of the River Leven. The river drains Windermere, the gorge was formed perhaps 15,000 years ago when meltwaters from a vast glacial lake forced a way through the low-lying ridge at the foot of what is now Windermere. The impressive falls visible are partially old weirs, once used to divert water to run turbines in waterside mills including the Blue Works, where the familiar "Dolly Blue" laundry product was produced until the works closed down in 1981. Paralleling the river is the southern end of the Lakeside and Haverthwaite Railway, the remaining section of the old Lakeside to Ulverston line now preserved as a steam railway, connecting with the seasonal boats, which ply Windermere. Haverthwaite Station is right alongside the A590 road.

A short walk down the lane brings you to a bridleway, signed left down the driveway to Trundle Brow. Follow this in front of the farm and cottages to the spot where the driveway sweeps left. Here go ahead through the bridleway gate, joining a wide path which soon enters woodland, dotted with some magnificent old broad-leaved trees. Simply remain with the bridleway to its end at the hamlet of Low Wood where the old mill, its mill race still intact, now houses a glass engravers and other small industrial concerns. Turn right through the hamlet, and right at the main road to cross the river bridge. Continue up along the road, keeping left at the junction you'll soon reach houses.

This is the main village area of Haverthwaite, strangely detached from the church, the other part of the village and the railway station. Walk up through to the sharp bend marked by chevrons. Here, go ahead up the narrow lane beside Pump Cottage. In about 50 yards bear left in front of Vernon Cottage. The grassy drive peters out into a walled pathway between field and wood, undulating gently along the woodland edge. In about 300 yards pass a wooden field gate on your left, and then bear right at the fork, rising with the path into the woods. You'll know if you're on the right track, as you'll soon pass by a solid old slab of slate still pierced by long disused gate hangings.

The wide walled track winds through this peaceful woodland liberally dotted with old yews and a haven for birds. It's just the sort of woodland where you may get a glimpse of red squirrels. Keeping left the path narrows and falls downslope to the woodland edge. As the open fields come into view, look carefully on your left for a wooden gate well hidden below thorn and hazel trees – there is a yellow waymark arrow on the gatepost. Once through this gate stick to the right-hand edge of this rough pasture, scrubby woodland to your right. Near the far end, pick your way through a boggy section and rise up to the edge of the woods, keeping these on your right to reach a stile. A distinct path leads ahead through the gorsey pasture, views opening out to the right to the high Coniston Fells including Coniston Old Man, once the highest point in Lancashire. Beyond the next stile the path continues to a ladder stile and a footbridge over a drainage ditch. Climb the bank beyond to gain the top of the embankment and turn right to return to the main A590. Turn left across the bridge and carefully cross to return to the Rusland Pool Hotel and the Saddle Bar.

Walk 2. Selside & Whinfell Tarn

Route: Selside – Rossil Bridge – Whinfell Tarn – Patton Mill

Terrain: Field paths & back lanes; some stiles can be very slippery

Distance: 6 miles

Start: The Plough Inn, Selside. Large car park adjoins

Map: O.S. Outdoor Leisure Sheet "The English Lakes, (SE)"

Access: The Plough stands beside the A6 about 4 miles north of Kendal.

The Plough Inn (01539 823687)

Originally a farmhouse, the main business became catering for travellers when the old pack and drovers road between Penrith and Kendal was turnpiked in 1763. The newly founded inn provided not only victuals for the passengers but also respite for the teams of horses which had hauled coaches up the steep incline from Kendal. It's now one of only a small handful of coaching inns that survive along the A6 in Cumbria, this once busy road having long lost most of its traffic to the M6, snaking its way up the Lune valley some miles to the east. A few tables on the cobbled forecourt of the Plough offer an ideal resting post at the end of a walk, the curving foreground pastures falling away to reveal truly stunning views across to the Pennines in the guise of the imposing flanks and upland commons of the Howgill Fells. Immediately behind the Inn are the shoulders of hills guarding the entrance to the hidden valley of Bannisdale.

Within the long, low, whitewashed pub is a single bar serving one large main lounge, with a separate games area. Well kept Tetley's bitter is the one regular draught beer, supplemented during busier times of year with one or two guest ales, usually from some of the better known national breweries. The Plough has an excellent reputation for good food, anything from simple bar snacks to restaurant fare, and if you're particularly taken by this undervisited, peaceful and scenic part of the Lakeland fringes then you can stay at the Inn for a night or two. Opening

hours are 11am to 3pm and 6pm to 11pm, Mondays to Fridays, 11am to
11pm Saturdays and 12 noon to 10.30pm Sundays.

The Walk

Just a few yards up the A6 from the car park, and on the other side of the
road, a footpath sign points to Selside School and Rossil Bridge. Climb
the stile here; it's a stone step stile and, in common with similar ones
throughout this walk, may be slippery in wet weather. Walk around the
left hand lip of the hollow in the field to reach the concreted farm drive,
here looking for the waymarked stile over the wall. Beyond this head
down the field to another step stile some yards to the left of the field
gate, then continue to the gate ahead leading into the end of the farmyard. Keep within and alongside the fence on the left of the farmyard to
reach another gate well to the left of the farmhouse, leaving the yard
here to walk along a field road. Remain with this past another gate and
up the field to the gate beneath a stand of sycamores. The way now is
alongside the wall on your left. Ahead is a striking view along the summits of the hills of Whinfell Common, the easternmost one being
Whinfell Beacon; further in the distance are the great saddlebacks of the
Howgill Fells.

A walker's gate in the field corner leads to an initially boggy field.
Keep the wall to your right for about 100 yards then angle gradually left
to the gate in the far left corner below a large sycamore. Walking now
between a wall (left) and a brook, continue ahead as the wall cuts away,
heading towards the bottom end of the copse ahead. Well before the
trees you'll come to a field road, turn right along this, ford the brook and
trace this track to the barn. Turn left along the tarred lane here and remain with it for about 400 yards to reach a junction near a bridge. Look
directly in front for the old packhorse bridge beneath the trees (N.B. not
the road bridge), a footpath sign bears the legend Guestford. Go through
the field gate immediately over the pack bridge then bear left alongside
the fence-cum-hedge. Simply trace the edge of this long field for about
600 yards to reach a new wooden stile about 200 yards past the narrow
point of the field. Leap over the brook beyond this then follow it upstream to the farm. A small gate leads to steps down to the brook, recross
it and walk up to the farmyard, then turn left and follow the rough drive
up to the road junction.

Turn sharp right along the narrow lane and walk along this the 300

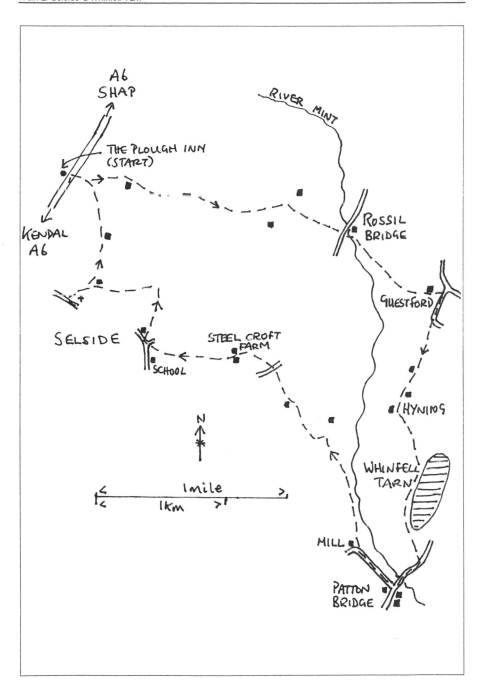

or so yards to the sharp left bend. In the corner of the wall here is a waymarked stile. Climb this into the steep pasture and walk downhill to the sharp offset corner of the wall pointing towards you. Here are a concrete stepped stile over the wall and a waymark arrow, both difficult to spot until you're almost upon them. Now keep to the lower level of the pasture to pass through the gateway in the wall at the far end, from where go ahead and right to the gated green lane, tracing this to the farmyard at Topthorn Farm. Go through the farmyard, farmhouse to your immediate right, and pick up the surfaced lane out of the yard.

The lane winds and dips for about a quarter of a mile to and past the farm at Hyning, then passes above the shore of the peaceful Whinfell Tarn. Cross the cattle grid and simply remain with the lane to its end, turning right here to drop to the old Patton Bridge. Immediately across this turn right along the road signposted for Selside Watchgate. In about a quarter of a mile the road bends left. Leave it here and walk ahead along the footpath signposted for Whitwell Folds, passing beside the medieval mill here at Patton Mill, dated on the nameboard from 1246 but long since converted into a comfortable country house. The path follows a route between the mill leat and the energetic River Mint, which has its source high up in hidden Bannisdale amidst the fells behind The Plough Inn. Here, the river has carved a course down across a series of rock shelves resulting in a delightful set of low waterfalls in the midst of woods.

Remain with the waterside path to a stile, once over which cut left to miss out the bend in the river and find another stile on your left beneath a hazel tree, about 30 yards before the corner of the field. Rejoin the riverside path, soon passing above the weir feeding the mill leat. Once over the next stile allow the river to curve off to the right, instead following the path around the ledge in the hillside to reach a complicated set of walls and fences near the field corner. Your route is waymarked by an arrow on a gatepost on your right, follow the direction indicated to crest the bank within the pasture, continuing to the wall at the far side. Take your time to find the stone step stile over this wall - essentially where the wall crest is slightly lower - and walk down the field beyond keeping the fence on your left. The views from this point are again impressive, the distant great wall of the Howgills and the Pennine ridge gouged as if by the action of a giant ice cream scoop.

Pass through the gate on your left and follow the line of hedge on your left to the next field corner. Don't pass through either of the gates

The Howgill Fells from Whitwell

here, and ignore the waymark arrow. Rather, turn right and trace the wall down to a narrow footbridge across a stream, once over which pick a way through the very boggy little field to the walkers gate at the far side. Climb the bank to the farm road and turn left along this, winding with it past the farm at High Biggersbank to reach a lane at a corner. The way is now through the gate opposite, a footpath sign here pointing the way to Selside School. Cross the first pasture to a squeeze stile beside the wooden-railed gap in the wall, then sight the farm in the middle distance and head for this, negotiating the craggy, marshy pasture as best you can. A walled farm lane leads from this pasture to the farmyard, leave this to the left of the farmhouse and simply follow the driveway all the way to the tarred lane just above Selside school.

Turn half-right here (N.B. *not* along the surfaced road to Candy Slack Farm) and walk the short distance to the white cottage. Just before reaching this is, on the right, a set of steps leading up to a stile and a footpath sign for Rossil Bridge and the A6. Walk up behind the cottage and along the obvious track in the pasture to pass through the gap in the wall at the field head, then keep the hedge on your left. The next obvious feature is a ladder stile on your left. About 15 yards before you reach this, however, is a narrow squeeze stile, right at the end of the hedge. Pass through this and head half left to the obvious deep little valley just below the trees. Walk down alongside the vigorous brook until it disappears into a culvert, at which point bear right along the line of wall, the path gradually developing into a green lane. Passing through several gates, the wall always to your left, then to both sides, brings you to a gate leading into the garden of a house. Walk ahead and then along the gravelled driveway to the left of the barn, emerging on the lane just uphill of Selside church. Turn left to this.

The part-rendered little St Thomas' Church is only about a century old, replacing earlier ones standing on this site or close by since roughly the time of the Civil War. Photographs and engravings of two earlier churches dating back to 1706 are on a wall inside, the list of incumbents goes back a further half-century or so. In the valley below and on the opposite side of the lane is the sturdy old manor of Selside Hall, reputedly built as a pele tower in the 1300s and redeveloped in its current guise in Elizabethan times.

Return to the gravelled driveway and walk back to the house. Just before the gate by which you originally entered the garden is a much smaller gate to your left. Go through this, walk across the craggy pasture passing immediately right of the electricity pole and go through the gate. Head now towards the farm, but pass to the left of all the buildings to the gate hosting a waymark arrow. Pick up the concreted drive here and turn left along it, following it for nearly half a mile. About 100 yards before reaching the main A6 you'll find, on your right, the waymarked stile crossed virtually at the start of the walk. Look left here to the pub, walk along the right-hand lip of the dip in the pasture and return to the high stone step stile, the main road and a pint at The Plough.

Walk 3. Bletherbarrow & Oxen Park

Route: Spark Bridge—Stock—Bletherbarrow Lane—Oxen Park—Colton

Terrain: One climb, lanes & field paths, some boggy sections

Distance: 7 miles

Start: The Royal Oak, Spark Bridge. Large car park adjoins

Map: O.S. Outdoor Leisure sheet "The English Lakes, (SE)"

Access: Spark Bridge is signposted off the A5092 some 5 miles north of Ulverston and 2 miles north of Greenodd, the pub is in the village centre.

Public transport: Infrequent weekday bus service 522 from Ulverston.

The Royal Oak (01229 861006)

Situated just up from the riverside village green in the hamlet of Spark Bridge, the pub is a relatively new use of an older building. Behind the solid, end-of-terrace building and car park, a small beer garden dots the high bank above the River Crake, beyond which are the gaunt, surprisingly complete remains of an old bobbin mill, once a thriving industry in these southern Lake District valleys. This mill, the last to survive in the Lake District, closed in the 1970s, the demand for bobbins – used in the cotton industry – disappearing along with much of the industry which made Lancashire famous. (The old bobbin mill at Low Stott Park, north of Newby Bridge, is now a working heritage attraction).

The Oak's split-level main room is comfortably appointed, part wood panelled, its walls hung with myriad "country" prints, clocks and brasses. Solid beams cross the ceiling, supported on walls of exposed stone, the whole area dotted with an eclectic mix of tables and chairs. Adorning the bar are handpumps dispensing Tetleys and Boddingtons bitters, augmented by another beer from a rotating list of goodies including Marstons Pedigree and Wadworth's 6X. Bar meals include locally caught salmon and trout as well as a wide selection of sweets to help replace those calories lost during the walk's exertions. Children are welcome. Opening hours are 11am-3pm and 5.30pm-11pm Mondays to Saturdays, 12 noon-10.30pm on Sundays.

The Walk

Walk down to the bridge and cross the River Crake. Ignore the first narrow road to the left and walk on a few paces to the next junction, here turning left up the steep Colton Hill road. Remain with this for about half a mile, ignoring the bridleway signs to left, then right. Crest the hill and commence a gradual descent, within about 200 yards look on the left for a bridleway sign indicating the route through a field gate. The field road beyond this gate rises gradually across the rough pasture, joining the line of a wall on your left. Views already open out to the jumble of peaks to the north of Windermere whilst closer to are the wooded lower hills of the Furness Fells. Off to the west (left) are the white growths of the wind turbines on Kirkby Fell/Lowick High Common, an eye-catching feature from almost all vantage points throughout the south of Lakeland.

Stay with the wall-side path for the best part of a mile. As the path drops into a hollow and the views momentarily disappear behind localised grassy knolls, look for the wooden gate in the field corner just a few yards below a wire fence. Go through this waymarked gate and stride ahead along the fenced pasture to another waymarked gate about 100 yards distant. Beyond this, further gates bring you to the farmyard of Sayles Farm. The way through the yard is marked by a low waymark post, essentially you aim to leave the yard along the rough roadway between the stone barn and the wooden stable block. The gate out of the farmyard is (September 1998) rather fallen on its hinges and difficult to open and close, so persevere! Wind with the stony field road beyond, in about 100 yards or so coming to another low waymark post directing you half-left off the roadway. The spectacular horizon of the Coniston Fells is soon revealed, the line of route being directly towards the conical summit of Coniston Old Man.

The next gate to take is maybe 50 yards in from the field corner, beyond this simply walk across the pasture in the direction of the distant farm, gaining the narrow Bessy Bank Lane along which turn left. Within 100 yards turn right along the walled driveway to Hill Park Farm. Here again are waymark arrows to the fields beyond; you leave the farmyard at the far end of the breeze-block and weatherboard barn, picking up a walled old track which acts, in all but the driest weather, as a stream bed. This fades to an initially grassy track up a long, narrow pasture. Ignore the footpath signed to the left, continuing easily uphill, the wall soon transferring to your right. This may be a particularly boggy stretch,

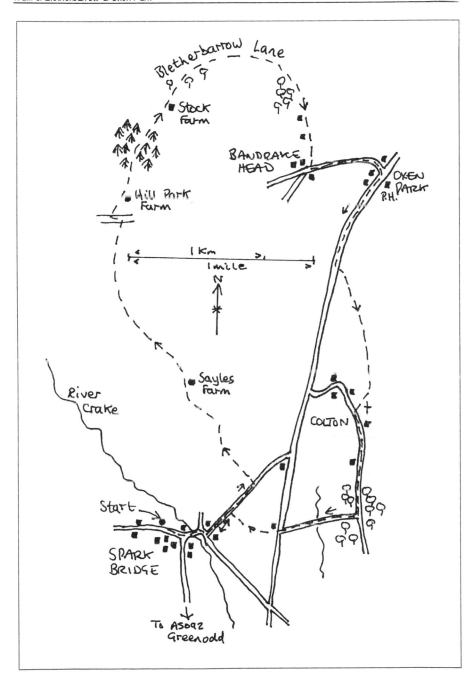

but the path eventually levels out across drier pasture to a gate through the wall at the top of the field. From here, sight the gateway into the distant woodland and walk to this, the rough pasture here particularly rich in harebells, yarrow and buttercups.

The stretch through the plantation of spruces is rather sombre. The path is obvious, keep ahead along the firebreak, ignoring the path off to the right from the glade you'll reach about half way through the woodland. There is wildlife to be seen here, keep your eyes peeled and ears alert for the shrill "pipping" sound of the goldcrest, one of the smallest British birds, which makes a home in the greener canopy of the tops of the close-packed trees. Tumbled walls in the trees to your left evidence the former use of these upland acres as walled sheep pastures. A bridle gate leads out of the woods and into a long narrow pasture, distant views shortly opening to the left to the Dunnerdale Fells and the curvaceous summits of Black Combe and White Combe, the outermost mountains of the Lake District.

Keep the wall on your left and walk to the distant farm at Stock. A signpost points the way through the farmyard and along the driveway beyond to reach a T-junction at the edge of a wood. Turn right along the tarred lane, which almost immediately deteriorates to a stony old fell road. This is Bletherbarrow Lane, an ancient route across the ridge between the Crake and Rusland Pool valleys. Stay with this for over half a mile. Just beyond the first gate you come to, bear right along the major track, signposted for Ickenthwaite. Views all round from this pleasant upland roadway are most pleasing, with vistas opening up to the south down to the great sands of Morecambe Bay, a view almost constantly with you for the next couple of miles.

Remain with the stony road to and through the gate beyond the beck. A few paces uphill, then bear right along the bridlepath signposted through the high bracken. This rises and falls beside pleasant oakwoods for several hundred yards before these peel away to the right, clothing the banks of the lively beck. The well-defined bridlepath continues southwards, heading all the time towards the distant, white-washed farmhouse. En route there are a number of gates to negotiate, and the route can prove boggy in places. The easiest way to negotiate these is to tread on the tufts of the thick reeds which thrive in these flushes – they give remarkably firm footing.

The walk reaches the farmyard at Abbot Park Farm. Go through this and join the drive, remaining with this for about half a mile, passing by the whitewashed house to eventually emerge onto a narrow road in the hamlet of Bandrake Head. The way now is left, tracing this winding lane across Colton Beck and up into the hamlet of Oxen Park. This characterful settlement boasts amongst its wide variety of buildings an increasingly rare corrugated iron village hall, several cottages dating back to the late 1600s, the welcoming Manor House pub and the old Black Lion House opposite, presumably once another beerhouse in this tiny place. With the pub to your left walk out from Oxen Park along the "main" road, descending gradually with it for about a quarter of a mile. Look on the left for a wide old gate, together with a footpath sign pointing the route to Colton. Trace this path along the line of old wall, then roughly along the obvious terrace around the hillside. Your target, Colton church, soon comes into view. This lies a further four gates away, the third of which is a particularly narrow and difficult one.

Colton's Holy Trinity church dates from the 1500s, much restored in the 1880s. Inside the whitewashed interior, sheltered by a solid wood-beamed roof, the marks on the font are said to be the result of parishoners in centuries past using it as a whetstone to sharpen swords, knives and scythes. The church stands in a churchyard far too large for the community it lies within, just a few farms and cottages. The reason for the mass of gravestones and memorials is that All Saints acts as the church for several parishes hereabouts spread over the low fells, including Bouth and Oxen Park.

Leave the church down along the narrow, tarred lane, following this to the sharp hairpin bend just above the farm about 250 yards away. The way here is left, past the farm and along the occasionally pitted, tarred lane for nearly a mile, passing en route a single farm. Just through the first area of woodland turn right at the junction and trace this lane to and over the bridge across Colton Beck, continuing beyond (ignore the bridleway sign to the left) to rise to a road. Pass through the gateway immediately opposite and keep the wall on your right, this bridlepath eventually narrowing to a passage between thorn trees before emerging into open pasture, wall now on your left. A short downhill section leads to a gate onto a minor road. Turn left and walk downhill to return to Spark Bridge along the same route on which you set out a few hours ago.

Walk 4. Blawith Knott

Route: Grizebeck — Well Wood — Giant's Grave — Blawith Knott — Ashlack Hall

Terrain: Easy walking on farm roads, open common and back lanes

Distance: 5½ miles

Start: The Greyhound Inn, Grizebeck. Car park opposite, lane adjacent.

Map: O.S. Outdoor Leisure sheet "The English Lakes, (SW)"

Access: The Greyhound Inn lies immediately beside the junction of the A5092 and A595 roads about 3 miles south-east of Broughton in Furness.

The Greyhound Inn (01229 889224)

There's not much to Grizebeck besides the Inn, a few cottages and houses, a small chapel and a garage on a rise near where the rushing Grize Beck loses itself in the mosses and marshes of Kirkby Pool, a part of the complex estuary of the River Duddon. The Inn, a solid, three storey Georgian building, was the precursor to the village garage, acting as a staging post on the old packhorse route between Millom and Greenodd. The buildings immediately behind the Greyhound were the ostler's house and stabling, used first by the jaggers in charge of the trains of packhorses, later by coachmen on the turnpike here at the foot of the formidable hill up to and across Kirkby Moor. The stables catered for the needs of the livestock, the Greyhound opened to cater for their owners.

The floor of the bar room is laid with enormous slabs of dark-blue slate, doubtless from the nearby Kirkby slate quarries, now largely disused but once comprising the largest slate quarries in England. The one bar serves a warren of separate areas within the public area, including dining room, pool room, back snug and lounge, several of which are warmed in winter by wood-burning stoves. The solid old beams give some idea as to the pub's age, more-so does the incredibly warped bar top, a lengthy cut of oak presumably there since the inn first opened and installed unseasoned, hence the alarming twisting of the wood. Let go of your pint pot at your peril.

This pint pot may hold a variety of beers, John Smiths bitter is the standard, joined by guests from all over the country, including beers from local Cumbrian and Lancastrian (this was, after all, once a part of Lancashire) breweries, Mitchell's of Lancaster for example. Drink these between 12 noon and 3pm and 6pm to 11pm (10.30pm Sundays), occasionally also open throughout the weekend days. A good selection of bar meals (including vegetarian) is also on offer up to 2pm and 9pm respectively. A pleasant spot is in the little beer garden behind the Inn, just yards from the Crize Beck and in front of the village post office stores, part of the Inn and open 3 days a week. The Greyhound (no-one knows why it has this name) also has a number of comfortable letting bedrooms.

The Walk

There are potentially some short, very boggy stretches along the route between Tenterbank and Hill farms near to the start of the walk.

Turn right from the Greyhound and bear left along the byroad in front of the garage. Join the busy main road and walk down to and over the tiny Prees Beck. Cross the road in this dip and walk uphill to the surfaced lane on the right, immediately below the retaining wall of the old village school. Turn right along this, the sounds of the main road soon fading as the lane rises across a steepening slope. Pass by the cottages at Tenterbank Farm and leave the yard through the wide gate in the end wall. Trace this walled lane, which may be very miry, and simply stick with it as it winds gently uphill, passing through gates as necessary and keeping the wall on your left as the lane fades to reach the abandoned farm and barns at Well Wood. Pass through this complex and rejoin the walled lane, rising to the point where it opens out slightly at the top end of Kirkby Park Wood, a few rowans and pines all that's left of this cleared forest.

Cresting the rise at this point opens out the view northwards to the heights of the Coniston group of mountains and westwards across the crinkly Dunnerdale Fells and shapely Caw to the long ridge of Corney Fell and the Combes. At the far side of this open area are three gates, you should take the central one and fall gradually with this sometimes rather overgrown lane down to the stile beside a gate. Once over this trace the rather stonier narrow walled track down to the yard of another abandoned farm at Far Houses. The roofless ruin still retains glass in the windows, old barns act as cattle byres and machinery moulders beneath ash and elder. It may be very boggy just beyond here. Go through the gate and keep the wall on your right to reach another gate on your right. Pass through this and walk to the farm in the middle distance beyond the trees, Hill Farm. Follow the driveway from here the quarter-mile or so up to the minor road at a crossroads.

Go straight over, then in a few paces bear left at the bridleway sign. Within a few steps bear right up the steeper grassy track through the bracken. Curve left with this in about 100 yards or so, leaving a steeper path climbing off to your right. A long gentle ascent along this wide grassy path through the bracken follows. In about 400 yards is a crossing of paths a short way below an outcrop of rocks. Keep ahead here, still climbing slowly. Ignore the steeper path off to the right to soon reach a point where the summit ridge of Blawith Knott comes into view. An easy walk along this winding bridleway will eventually bring you to a minor road crossing the moors here above Subberthwaite Common. The way is finally ahead along the signposted bridleway, but first turn left and cross the road. Just beyond the stream is a small chambered tomb, a bronze age burial site known as Giant's Grave, essentially one slab balanced on two others. From here an obvious path rises quite steeply to the summit of Blawith Knott with its distant views, not a dedicated public right of way but one well trodden for many years past. Only just over 800 feet above sea level, the views all round are exceptional, taking in virtually all the major summits of Lakeland and with distant views to the line of the Pennines and the famous Three Peaks of the Yorkshire Dales.

Return the same way to Giant's Grave and walk back up the road the few paces to the bridleway crossing, here turning left along it. In about half a mile a stony track goes off sharply back to the right, follow this to the farm entrance at the isolated Birch Bank Farm, here joining the driveway. This reaches a minor road. Turn right, walk the few paces past the old milk churn stand then go left along the road. The bulk of Great Burney is the hill immediately ahead, a little further distant are some of the wind turbines on Kirkby Moor, just above the slate quarries beneath which stands The Greyhound Inn.

Ignore the first surfaced lane on the right and continue about half a mile to the next. Turn along it and wind across the common to the entrance to the farm complex at Knittleton. The way is left immediately

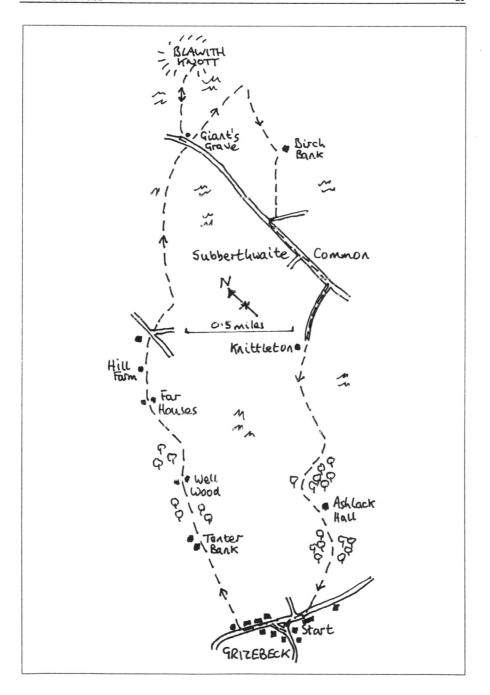

before the large semi-corrugated iron barn. Pass through the gate and go
the few paces to another, tumbledown one. Go through this and pick up
the line of wall to your right, the farmhouse now off down to your right.
Stay with this grassy fieldside road to the end of the rough open pasture
fringing Heathwaite Fell. Pleasant views soon open out ahead down the
length of the Duddon Estuary. At the end of the wall are two gates, go
through the left-hand one and trace the line of the wall on your right for
about 100 yards to a gate on the right some way before the trees. Go
through this, beside a large thorn tree, and go ahead up the field road
(ignore the lesser track to the left and falling downslope). This becomes
more distinct as it winds across the rough, gorse and thorn tree infested
pasture. It joins a more obvious dirt roadway. Drop down this to reach
the yard beside the barns and stables at Ashlack Hall, its splendid old
façade and the typical Lakeland chimneystacks – tall, rounded, rendered – visible along the drive in a short distance. Pick up the driveway
here and follow it right down to the main road at the edge of Grizebeck.
The Greyhound is across the road and to the right.

Ashlack Old Hall

Walk 5. In Dunnerdale

Route: Broughton Mills—Hovel Knott—Ulpha—Ulpha Park—Beckfoot

Terrain: Some steep ascents and descents; sheep tracks, back lanes, woodland

Distance: 7 miles

Start: The Blacksmith's Arms, Broughton Mills. Small car park next to pub.

Map: O.S. Outdoor Leisure sheet "The English Lakes, (SW)"

Access: The pub is about 2.5 miles north-east of Broughton in Furness. Take the A593 Coniston road from Broughton Market Place and fork left In about 1.5 miles at the sign for Broughton Mills.

The Blacksmith's Arms (01229 716824)

This is the quintessential tiny country pub. The Blacksmith's seems largely to have been caught in amber since the year dot (or 1748 when it was licensed), retaining all that is sought in a country pub, the sort of place that Hilaire Belloc or G. K. Chesterton would have waxed lyrical about in the early 1900s as being, even then, a part of bucolic England.

Hidden within a maze of single-track lanes, it adjoins a working farmyard and nestles above a lively river beneath crinkly, shapely fells, their ever-changing hues complemented by the myriad greens and russets of the bracken and woodland dappling the hill and valley sides. Ducks and chickens scratch in the car park and on the cobbled forecourt, the village trough is opposite. The most modern feature of the pub (apart from electricity and a small car park...) must be the Victorian post box set into the pub's front wall. The whitewashed building contains an entrance passageway off which lie 2 small rooms, the one to the left half-filled by an enormous old cast-iron black-leaded range, complete with ovens, spice cupboard and (in winter) roaring fire. The tables and solid, almost medieval, wall benches within leave enough room to allow customers to spend a cosy, convivial hour or two over a few jars or some of the splendid food (the only real concession to modernity in generations of service to the community) for which the newish owners have gained a wide reputation. The room to the right, equally small and hosting the bar, is somewhat more airy and light, with window seats beneath mullioned windows and another fire to mull any pints left unguarded in the grate.

The current owners have made a few changes since commencing their tenure. Two more rooms have been opened out to create dining areas, although you wouldn't realise they were there as you enter. "The Shop" is secreted behind the bar, created from what was the former mill hamlets' shop. A further, slightly larger room lies at the back of the pub, probably the old farm's best parlour now reborn as a dining room, in much the same character as the main front room. All the rooms can be, and in winter often are, lit by gas lighting.

The Blacksmith's is open all day every day, 12 noon-11pm (10.30pm Sundays). For the drinker the main attraction is the pleasant Blacksmith's Best Bitter specially brewed for the pub by Derwent Brewery. Theakstons Bitter is the other regular draught offering and the spare handpump dispenses any of a variety of beers sourced by the owner, often a seasonal brew.

For the local it's maybe a rather sedate, quiet local, enlivened by events such as the hunt meets or the annual Marrow Championship held each autumn for many years past. For the visitor and pub purist, it's a rare treat, rivalled only, perhaps, by The Blue Ship in deepest West Sussex, The Star at Netherton in the heart of Northumberland, Staffordshire's Anchor Inn at High Offley or a few isolated old pubs in the Marches of Herefordshire. Miss it at your peril!

The Walk

This may not be the longest walk in this book but it's probably the most energetic, with several steep ascents and descents across the southern ridge of the Dunnerdale Fells. I'd not recommend doing the walk after prolonged or heavy summer rain as parts of the way are through long tracts of high bracken, which can be damnably wet!

Turn downhill from the pub and keep left, passing the old corn mill to cross the hump-backed bridge over the River Lickle, then take the "Dead End" lane up beside the cottage. On reaching Green Bank Farm turn right up the lane the few paces to Greenbank Cottage. The way is to the left immediately in front of the cottage, there's a low bridleway sign here. Keep the wall on your left and rise with the stony track through the woods. At the top end of the woods keep left alongside the wall and continue to climb to the corner marked by, of all things, a picnic table, a strange artefact, you may think, until turning to enjoy the panorama down the length of the Duddon Estuary.

Turn left around the corner here and stay with the grassy bridlepath beside the wall, favouring the right-hand course at the split (although the two paths shortly join again). Crest the rise and there's a super view ahead of the knotty landscape so typical of these Dunnerdale Fells; Hovel Knot and Great Stickle are the two prominent hills in view from this point. At the junction keep left, drop down the walled track and cross the small pasture to the wooden bridleway gate beyond Sticklelongue Beck. Once through this walk on to pass above the tree-shaded old stone barn down to your left. Pass through the next gate, turn left and walk to the very large ash tree. About 50 paces beyond this take the steep, narrow path which forks to the right through bracken.

This path gains height quickly to pass through the col (dip) between Hovel Knott and Little Stickle. Wade with the path slightly right through the bracken to reach the wider, green bridlepath. Bear right with this and then bend left, leaving a lesser path to rise to the higher crags of Great Stickle and Stickle Pike. Views open out ahead to the clean, high sweep of Black Combe and, to the right of this, the heights of Whitfell and Corney Fell. Stay with the wide bridlepath as it courses above the flat, marshy looking area to your right. To the left the bracken infested slopes ruffle over low crags and lose height to become upland pastures. A few twists and turns and the deep vale of the River Duddon fully opens out at your feet. Simply stick with the bridleway as it descends gradually, sometimes a little steeply, to the valley floor road. Turn right along this and remain with it for the long mile to the bridge at Ulpha. Along the way, look up to the right for a most endearing view of the lower crags cloaked in a mixed woodland of yews, juniper, rowan, ash, sessile oak and birch trees.

On reaching Ulpha cross the bridge and turn left along the road signed as a fell road to Bootle. *(Ulpha is an alternative possible start for this walk, as there is off road parking on the east side of the bridge near to the junior school or above the river – and the Blacksmith's Arms would be a welcome break part way round!).* The scattered houses and cottages of the hamlet dot the valley floor, but the pub that was a favourite of Edwardian trippers has long closed its doors. Stay with the road for a good half mile to reach the imposing house on the left, modestly named as a cottage. Just beyond this cross the beck to the old mill, its chimney now long out of use, with a small fir tree growing out of its top. This was an old bobbin mill, one of up to 100 or so which supplied turned-wood bobbins to the cotton and textile industries of Britain and the Empire.

Opposite the mill, on your left, the way is signposted as a footpath through the gate and along the stony lane. Keep left at the fork, remaining alongside the wooded beck. Pass through the bottom gate and the woods are temporarily left behind. Views to your left up the Duddon are interrupted by the great lump of Wallowbarrow Crag, beyond which some of the giants of the heart of the Lake District loom, whilst to your right the Dunnerdale Fells catch the sunlight amongst the crags. The track curves to the right and traces a wall across the foot of stony pastures.

Cast your eyes up to the right and you should spot a ruined building on the top of a crag above the woods. This was Frith Hall, a hunting lodge used by guests of the Huddlestone family, Lords of the Manor in the 1600s. Two centuries later it was in business as an inn on the packhorse road between Dunnerdale and Millom, the victim of a murder here is said to haunt the lonely ruins of this long-abandoned site. In the 1700s the establishment gained a certain notoriety as a wayside marriage hall, a sort of Gretna Green of the day where eloping couples plighted their troth.

Go through the gate into the woods, from which point it's a case of remaining with the woodland road for a good two miles. It's a very pleasant stroll, the mixed deciduous woodland littered with mossy boulders and alive with birdsong. In places there are stands of very tall larch, letting light into the occasionally gloomy woods as they climb the slopes of Ulpha Park.

The track, sometimes along the woodland edge, sometimes well within the woods, eventually reaches a small estate sawmill, the products of which are evident stacked outside, largely gates for such as the National Trust, the National Park and for use on the Duddon Estate, at the heart of which you now are. Immediately past the first sheds on your left look for the footpath sign pointing out the path left down into the trees, a path tracing the course of a beck down to the right. At the foot, turn right, cross the bridge and walk on to the solid, gabled house guarding one of the driveways to Duddon Hall. The way is left, through

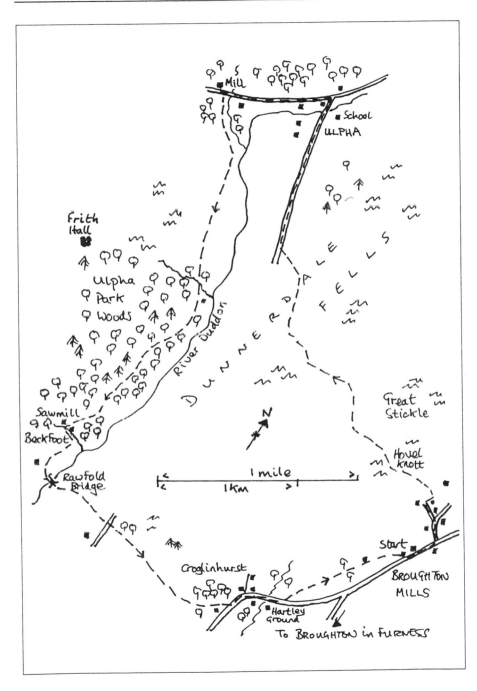

the kissing gate and along to Rawfold Bridge. This curves high above the cataracts and deep pools of the Duddon, which here has worn, over time, a series of potholes in the underlying rock, best seen immediately below the bridge to your right. It's a lovely sylvan setting, the roar of the falls adding to the sense of peace.

Go straight over the track beyond the bridge and enter the woods ahead via the gate. There's now a gentle climb up a wide rocky path, its route marked regularly by some enormous piles of pine needles, the nests of wood ants. It's worth spending a couple of minutes looking closely at the activity, you'll soon see scores of worker ants converging on the mound, each one carrying yet another single needle to add to the structure.

Go through the gate at the top of the woods, walk ahead a few paces then veer left to the stone step stile through the high wall. Above this follow the line of wall up to the head of the field where steps up the retaining wall and a small gate give access to the minor road. Cross straight over, climb up the awkward steps and stile directly opposite and commence a short but very steep scramble up the slope, keeping towards the right hand side of the copse of gnarled old oaks. Looking behind, the considerable mansion of Duddon Hall is clearly visible within its wooded setting above the river. Keep climbing beyond the trees to cross over a grassy field road. Continue to climb, passing either side of the knoll to come across a shallow upland valley. Look ahead to the firwoods peeking over the horizon. Trace with your eye the wall sweeping down towards you in an arc from here. It comes to a cross-wall in the hollow beyond the valley. The stile you need is about 75 yards up from where these two walls meet, a stone step stile marked by wooden posts.

Follow the path beyond through the high bracken to reach the lone sycamore in the dip in the ridge. From here walk ahead a few paces and the sudden deep vale of the Lickle is at your feet. The way is now straight down, a very steep descent through the bracken (along an obvious path) which falls to a wall at the break in slope. Turn left along the line of this, pass into the wood (Woodland Trust owned) and follow this woodland edge path within the trees, behind the cottage and down to the lane. Turn left and keep right at the junction, winding through the barns and farmhouses here at Croglinhurst to reach the bridge across the Lickle. Climb the road beyond this, pass by the cottages at Hartley Ground and stay with the lane to the stretch of metal fencing about 150 yards uphill.

Hovel Knot and Great Stickle – crinkly Dunnerdale Fells at their best

Take the footpath on the left signposted from the far end of this rail fencing and trace the threadbare line of the old hedgerow across the pasture (*N.B. not the roadside hedge*). Go through two stiles and slowly ascend to the top-right corner to another stile (it may be very boggy immediately beyond this). Now look across the pasture to the tallest beech tree in the middle distance and walk in line of sight to the right of this to reach another squeeze stile and tiny footbridge. Continue ahead from this to find a small gate marked with a waymark arrow. Past this walk up to the beeches and to the possibly unique path (gated) beneath the solid stone barn. This short passageway emerges into the courtyard in front of the splendid old whitewashed farmhouse of Lumholme. From here join the driveway and follow this to its end, passing through the gate beside an isolated house then winding through the delightful fold of cottages to hit the road just yards from the front door of the Blacksmith's Arms.

Walk 6. Kentmere Tarn

Route: Staveley – Park House – Staveley Head Fell – Kentmere Tarn – Scroggs Bridge

Terrain: Back lanes and cart tracks, one long, easy climb

Distance: 6½ miles

Start: The Station Hotel, Staveley – large car park.

Map: O.S. Outdoor Leisure sheet "The English Lakes, (SE)"

Access: Staveley is bypassed off the A591 between Kendal and Windermere. Turn off the bypass to the village centre, the railway station is signposted, the Hotel adjoins it.

Public transport: Staveley station is served by regular trains from Lancaster, Preston and Manchester. The 555 Kendal to Windermere/Ambleside/Keswick bus service passes through the village regularly every day from early morning to late evening (later start on Sundays).

The Station Hotel (01539 821385)

The branch line railway to Windermere opened in 1847; Staveley's Station Hotel was built some years later to cater for the increasing influx of visitors nurtured by the works of the Lakeland poets and writers. Comprehensively renovated and redecorated in 1997, the pub is now a comfortable small-town inn hosted by one of the most walker-friendly landlords you're likely to meet anywhere. If you're staying (3 letting rooms) then he'll drive you any distance to the far end of a linear walk (e.g. to Haweswater for the walk back across Harter Fell). If you do the walk suggested in this chapter and get rained on, then he'll dry off your clothes whilst you sit in front of the fire, wrapped in a blanket and steaming over a cool beer, maybe eating one of the pizzas available any time the pub is open.

It's a "Pubmaster" pub, the bar groaning under their standard range of lagers and smoothflow beers. Between the myriad illuminated fonts, however, are handpumps dispensing Wadworth's 6X and Boddingtons Bitter. Framed photographs of olden-day Staveley and surrounding areas line the walls, interspersed with a wide variety of odd artefacts, from shotguns to spears, fishing rods to various brass oddments – old fire extinguishers feature prominently. There's also a small collection of stuffed birds throughout the large, comfortable main room, whilst the stairwell walls hold a fine range of Victorian halters and related equine paraphernalia. The pool table and fruit machines are housed in a room well separated from the bar area, itself facing the open fire across the comfortably appointed, part-carpeted and slate floored lounge.

Opening hours depend on the day and season. Winter months, it's evenings only from 6pm – 11pm, all day weekends. During summer (say, May to October) the pub is also open at lunchtime on Wednesdays to Fridays, 12 noon to 3pm. Food hours are 12 noon – 1.45pm, and 6.30pm – 8.30pm; Pizzas (and coffee & tea) are available at any hour the pub is open – on some mornings you can get coffee from 10am.

Kentmere Tarn

The Walk

Turn right from the Hotel's door and walk past houses and cottages to find and cross the footbridge over the lively River Gowan, then turn left along Main Street (if you're doing this walk in winter, then the Eagle & Child Inn, 200 yards to your right, may well be open; Theakstons and a guest beer). Walk along to the squat tower of the old St Margaret's Chapel, standing alone in its graveyard; a plaque outlines the history of the medieval site. A footpath is signed to the right between the chapel and the car park of the Duke William Inn (Boddingtons & Flowers beers), follow this tarred, walled pathway past the well-tended bowling green to and over the footbridge across the River Kent. Go left through the squeeze stile beyond and trace the muddy path beside the river, soon passing above one of the village's two weirs, the solid, slate-built mill and works it fed still standing on the far bank. The footpath issues into a minor road, bear left and follow this to the junction just before Barley Bridge. Turn right (i.e. don't cross the bridge) and start the long, gradual climb up Hall Lane (signed as a no through road).

For the better part of a mile the lane rises gently past wooded slopes and steeper, rough pasture, the increase in altitude also improving the views west (left) to the crinkly summits of Hugill Fell and Black Crag. The lane's verges are remarkably wealthy in wild raspberry bushes, offering an unexpected feast during late summer; myriad other plants including the fragrant, creamy blooms of meadowsweet and the spear-like flowers of betony colour the banks. At the sharp hairpin bend keep left, the lane descending gradually towards Park House Farm. Leave this off to your left, the lane now deteriorating to a rough mountain road as it rises alongside a series of low waterfalls and rapids livening the flow of Hall Beck. Ahead, tantalising glimpses of the high fells at the head of Kentmere take the eye.

An isolated shepherd's hut shaded by a lone maple is the only sign of habitation in these rough upland pastures. Passing through the first gate, marked by a "Bridleway Only" sign, continue on through the next gate then pass through the first gateway on your left, about 40 yards before the complex of sheepfolds along the "main" road. This field road is much less obvious, if still easily identifiable. Climb gradually over the shoulder of the hillside, fine views unfolding to the north as this hill is crested. A clutch of peaks well over 2000 feet encircles the top end of the Kentmere valley. Reading from the east are Kentmere Pike, Harter Fell, Mardale Ill Bell, High Street, Thornthwaite Crag, Frostwick and Ill

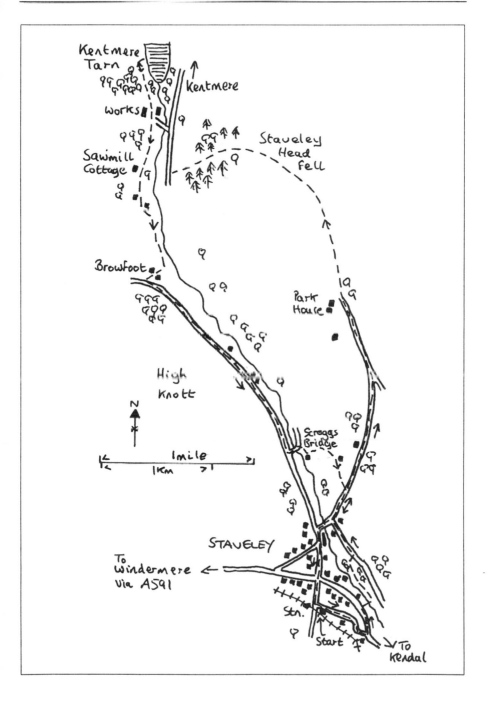

Bell – High Street is amongst the highest 20 or so summits in the entire National Park.

Go through the next gate and walk ahead about 20 paces to find an obvious crossways of tracks, the short grass spangled in summer with countless yellow flowers of tormentil. Turn left here and follow this bridleway, walking parallel to the wall on your left and soon entering a swathe of bracken. About 75 yards into the bracken keep right at the fork, tracing the wide track roughly along the level, soon crossing a boggy area on rough stepping stones. To your left is a low mound guarded by rusting fencing, the remains of long-exhausted small scale lead workings. The path soon begins to descend, the views up Kentmere to the lonely farms, old church and ancient Kentmere Hall gradually fading behind the foreground knolls. Simply remain with the path, passing gates as necessary, to gain a pass between two plantations of firs. Keep the left-hand of these woods immediately on your left and you'll eventually come to the minor road winding up the Kentmere valley. Turn right along this.

In about a quarter of a mile turn left over the bridge and along to the Hepworth Air Filtration works. The way back to Staveley is left, along the driveway to the pottery. It is, however, well worth diverting up the valley to enjoy the views across Kentmere Tarn. To do so turn right past the car park barrier (there are waymark arrows attached to the factory buildings) and walk through the long yard between the warehouses. A wide, muddy roadway leads from the far end of the yard into the woods. In about a quarter of a mile are ample opportunities to view Kentmere, framed by trees. There were once two lakes in the valley. The upper one, beyond the scattered hamlet of Kentmere, has silted up over thousands of years. The current lake has survived, to an extent, due to the extraction of diatomite, a silica-rich deposit of single-celled algae important in industrial filters (hence the long-established works), insulation materials and in metal polishes.

Return to the car park barrier and follow the lane to the Kentmere Pottery at the picturesquely situated Sawmill Cottage. The path leaves the gravelled yard to the left of the garage, a narrow, railed way leading to a slippery footbridge across Park Beck. Beyond this, and a gate, the path widens to become a walled greenway. Turn left at the T-junction and pass by two cottages, following the tarred driveway for several hundred yards. About 30 paces before reaching a bridge over the river, turn right, go through the gate and trace the rough old lane along a pleasant wooded stretch above the River Kent. The lane bends right and climbs to and through the few cottages and barns at Browfoot Farm. Continue beyond up the short, steeper incline to reach a tarred lane and turn sharp left along this.

Remain with this, the hardly used Browfoot Lane, for about a mile, a pleasant walk through copses and above hay meadows between the lane and the river. Look out for deer browsing in these meadows, you've every chance, too, of seeing buzzards and hearing the laughing call of green woodpeckers echoing from the enclosing, steep valley sides.

At the junction turn left across Scroggs Bridge, then go immediately right along the rough driveway to the old mill cottages. The footpath passes behind these cottages, look for a large white arrow painted onto a tree trunk and directing you left, across a stile and up the edge of the pasture. At the top a ladder stile leads into a sunken lane. Turn right and walk to and through the farmyard at Scroggs Farm, continuing along the long drive to the minor road. Turn right, and bear right at the end to cross Barley Bridge immediately below a substantial weir. Turn left at the junction and keep left at the village war memorial cross to reach the centre of Staveley. Go straight over the crossroads here, over the bridge across the River Gowan and along Station Road to return to The Station Hotel, about 250 yards distant.

Walk 7. Heugh Scar & Barton Church

Route: Tirril – Celleron – Heugh Scar – Pooley Bridge – Barton

Terrain: One gradual, easy climb; some potentially boggy moorland

Distance: 7½ miles

Start: The Queens Head, Tirril

Map: O.S. Outdoor Leisure sheet "The English Lakes, (NE)"

Access: Tirril is on the B5320, half-way between Eamont Bridge (Penrith) and Pooley Bridge, at the foot of Ullswater. Car park adjoins.

Public transport: The 108 bus runs infrequently, Mondays to Saturdays, between Penrith and Patterdale via Tirril. Also a daily post-bus (Mon-Sat) and summer Sunday buses.

The Queens Head (01768 863219)

This is surely one of Lakeland's unsung gems. The Queens has everything you'd expect from a village inn set within the sphere of influence of the Lakes idyll – oak beams, roaring fires, flagged floors, great beers, a certain antiquity and the compulsory Wordsworth connection. But as it's just off the tourist trail one thing it lacks is crowds of trippers. Whilst most visitors to Ullswater head for Patterdale or direct to Pooley Bridge via the main A592, the hamlets strung out along the B5320 retain a peaceful atmosphere.

The long, low, whitewashed pub dates from 1719, its quality gaining the protection of a Grade 2 listing from English Heritage. The features referred to above – beams, flagged floors etc. – are there in abundance in both of the bar rooms. The layout of the front bar is particularly characterful, the settles, posts, rafters and beams hung with myriad pewter tankards creating the feel of a snug around one of the old fireplaces. This atmosphere is emphasised by the general decor of the pub's interior, a glorious mix of black painted raw stonework, neutral colourwashed mellowed plaster and dark wood panelling of various

The Queen's Head at Tirril, a Wordsworth family home

gauges. A restrained collection of old brass spirit measures, plates, prints, etc. dapple the walls. The back bar, equally capacious, is the place to go for pub games.

In the early 1900s the pub, which was a licensed premises from the outset, was eventually extended into the adjoining cottage, an area now set aside as a restaurant. Apparently the licensees of the time had been trying to buy out the cottage owner for decades but, as she was a confirmed teetotaller, only the eventual visit of the grim reaper freed the property. Her ghost is said to haunt the building to this day! The range of food available both at the bar and in the restaurant is exceptional.

And the "compulsory" Wordsworth connection? A debenture held at the pub proves that one William Wordsworth became owner of The Queens Head in 1807, the building passing to him from his brother who died in that year and who had inherited the pub some years earlier. Previous generations of Wordsworths had moved to the area from Yorkshire, nearby Barton church has memorials to such. William Wordsworth remained the largely non-resident owner until 1836.

Which leaves just the beers to sample. The award as CAMRA Westmorland's Pub of the Season, 1998, all-but guarantees the consistent quality of the beer; the fact that the licensees hold a regular beer festival over the second weekend in August each year, featuring a dozen and more ales dispensed either by handpump or direct from the barrel perched on the bar-top adds to the attraction for the connoisseur. Badged outside as a Black Sheep Brewery pub, the Queens is in fact a free house. There's always Black Sheep Bitter on tap together with three other beers, almost always from the smaller local or regional breweries – Dent Brewery, Hesket Newmarket, etc. – rather than national or larger regional concerns. Opening hours are 12 noon-3pm and 6pm-11pm on Mondays to Fridays, all day (from 12 noon) at weekends. And if the heady combination of great beers, fine food and a bracing ramble encourage you to tarry a while, there are 7 letting bedrooms available at this most convivial village inn.

The Walk

Walk past the garage to find the village post office stores, immediately past which take the kissing gate on the right, a public footpath signed for Penrith. At the foot of this long cattle pasture a stile leads to a narrow, wooded path above a beck. This path reaches the village back lane beside a stone bridge. Cross this and walk uphill, soon passing a terrace of old cottages on your left. At the top of the hill the road bends sharp left at a junction whilst an estate road continues ahead into Quakers Lane. Continue ahead a few paces and take the narrow, tree-canopied bridlepath to the right of the road name-board, a potentially muddy route rising to a tarred lane beside a barn. Cross straight over, farmyard to your right, and remain with the bridlepath.

Off to your left is the solid old farmhouse of Thorpe Farm. Soon after you see this the track divides. Take the left-hand fork, the bridlepath narrowing as it arrows beneath mature ash trees; the way is sometimes awkward underfoot due to the exposed tree roots. Here and there, stands of meadowsweet and the occasional bloom of bellflower brighten the banks. The path emerges at a bend on the B5320, which can be fairly busy at the height of summer. Bear right along it, in a short distance passing by the impressive Kirkbarrow Farm then, shortly, the road to Barton Church. Don't go down this but, rather, look on the left for the signposted footpath to Celleron just a few paces further along the main road. Cross carefully and join the field-edge track, passing through the gate and leaving the barn off to your right.

Towards the head of the second field, the field elbows to the right beneath a small outcrop of limestone. Follow the hedge to find a stile

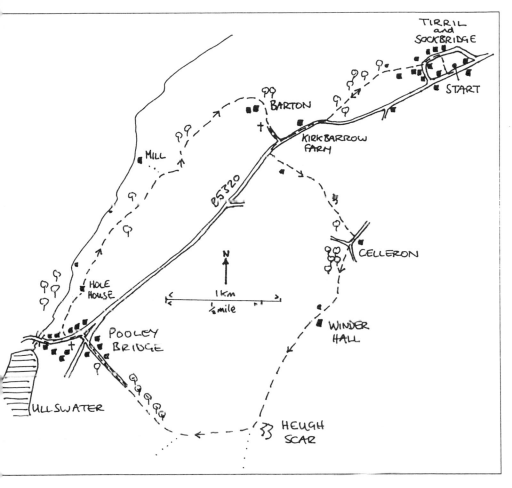

marked with a waymark arrow and a band of yellow tape/paint on the
hand post. Climb this and look upfield for a similarly marked stile, once
over which again look uphill for a yellow marker at the offset field corner. From here keep the hedge on your right, climbing gradually alongside a line of trees to a stile beside a field gate. Beyond this, turn right up
the lane to the T-junction here at Celleron.

The way is now through the field gate into the pasture virtually opposite this junction; there's a small "footpath" plaque attached to the
gate. The path rises gradually beside the spinney, fenced in to your
right. Off to the left the wide horizon is made up of the line of the high

Pennines, an impressive line of fells culminating in Cross Fell, at 2930 feet the highest of the Pennine summits. Climb the ladder stile at the head of the field and turn right along the farm lane. Go through the gate in front of the old cottage and walk past the sheep pens towards the entrance to the farmyard here at Winder Hall Farm. Before reaching this entrance, however, bear right with the rough lane and rise with this to a kissing gate beside a wooden field gate at the top end of the long, thin farmyard. Continue along the rough roadway beyond for about 100 yards, then bear right along a wide grassy path to roughly parallel the line of trees and wall off to your right. You should aim to pass just to the right of the right-hand most electricity pylon you can see.

The going may be a little boggy underfoot in places. As the wall on your right bends away, identify a grassy path across the gorsey moor and which heads for the little outcrop of limestone visible some distance away and half-left. Head for this, Heugh Scar, joining a wide and well used moorland road immediately below the rocks. Turn right along this and remain with it for about 200 yards. The views ahead improve with each step, almost the entire length of Ullswater stretching away beneath the sharp top of Arthur's Pike and, further on, Hallin Fell and Loadpot Hill high above the deep chasm of Fusedale. On the far, eastern bank the fells rise ever higher to the airy heights of Helvellyn, third highest of England's mountains at 3116 feet.

Bear right at the fork, marked by a small cairn of stones, soon passing above a reedy spring. This wide path slowly loses height; walk to the top end of the row of trees visible below and off to your right. Follow the outside of the wall here, the sycamores to your right, eventually falling tó the near end of a tarred road. Join this and follow it down off the fells to Pooley Bridge, going straight over the cross roads as you reach them. Bear left at the mini-roundabout to the village centre with its shops, three pubs and a National Park Information Centre.

The route out of Pooley Bridge is along the signposted footpath which passes immediately to the right of The Sun Inn and through the yard at the rear. Go through the kissing gate at the back of this and pick up the rough field road, remaining with this past the sewage plant and to and past the little slate-built gauge house beside the weir in the River Eamont. The steep, wooded slopes opposite clothe the conical hill of Dunmallard. Beyond the gauge-house follow the riverside path for a few paces then climb the distinct, narrow path up to the gate into the farmyard at Hole House Farm. Pass through the yard, between several barns now reborn as holiday cottages. At the far end pass to the left of the modern, corrugated iron barn and climb the stile beside a field gate to gain another well defined field road. Simply remain with this for about a half mile, passing through further gates/stiles as appropriate. The western horizon opens out beyond the wooded ridge above the Eamont to reveal some of the higher peaks of the northern end of the Lake District, Blencathra and Bowscale amongst them.

This field road reaches a gate virtually beneath some tall dead trees, just beyond which a kissing gate gives access to a bridlepath. Turn left along this, heading for Barton. Through the gate at the end follow the track, fence to your right, to a further gate, beyond which head half-left to a waymark post at the field edge. Again, here, follow the direction for Barton, winding with the path above a marshy brook to a stile at the field corner. In the field beyond the right of way loops across the middle to reach a double set of field gates in the far bottom-left corner. Once through these walk ahead for thirty paces then turn right along the wide field road, your route to Barton Church soon confirmed by a sign nailed to a large ash tree.

Follow this field road through to Barton Church Farm, climbing the ladder stile to gain the grounds of the large farmyard area. The route crosses a bridge over the brook, then passes some way to the left of the old farmhouse to approach the inner farmyard between corrugated iron barns. At the far side of the yard pass under the arched entrance beneath the long stone barn and follow the driveway away from Church Farm and to the left of the solid old stone Glebe Farm, the lintel stone dating it to the 1630s. The beech-hedged driveway winds round the gardens to eventually reach the lych gate to Barton's St Michael's Church. This remarkable old building retains much of its Norman architecture, particularly the squat tower which dominates the *inside* of the church, creating essentially a tunnel between the nave and chancel. On the chancel wall is a small brass plaque commemorating Richard Wordsworth, grandfather to the poet and also Anne Myers, the poet's aunt. Nearby there's also an impressive listing of vicars and rectors stretching back, with two shortish gaps in the early sixteenth and fifteenth centuries, to 1304.

Return to the drive and follow it to the main road, turning left along this. From here it is simply a matter of retracing the outward route in reverse, passing Kirkbarrow Farm to find the bridlepath on the left signposted for Thorpe, thence eventually down to the stream and the footpath on the right for Tirril.

Walk 8. Dacre & Dalemain

Route: Pooley Bridge – Maiden Castle – Dacre – Dalemain

Terrain: Gently undulating field paths, quiet back lanes

Distance: 5 or 6 miles

Start: Dunmallard Car Park, Pooley Bridge (west side of the bridge)

Map: O.S. Outdoor Leisure sheet "The English Lakes, (NE)"

Access: Pooley Bridge is at the foot (northern tip) of Ullswater, on the B5320 between Eamont Bridge (Penrith), Patterdale and Windermere (via A592)

Public transport: The 108 bus runs infrequently, Mondays to Saturdays, between Penrith and Patterdale via Pooley Bridge. Also a daily post-bus (Mon-Sat) and summer Sunday buses.

The Horse & Farrier, Dacre (017684 86541)

Every isolated rural hamlet should have a pub such as the Horse & Farrier. Indeed, most did until the 1960s when the dual curse of accountants and major brewery muscle precipitated the rapid decline of the country pub. So it's very pleasing to report that this increasingly rare example of a rural community pub is still thriving, combining excellent beers, fine food and community spirit (the Post Office sign beside the door is a clue...).

Originally two cottages built in about 1750, one was, from the outset, the hamlet's ale house, the other simply a farm cottage (or, maybe, given the name, part of a smithy). The one main pub room has a small bar at one corner and a considerable, blackened cast-iron range forming most of the wall at the other end. Solid beams support the low ceiling, crossing the room to a recessed, stone-mullioned window looking out to cottages and the squat tower of St Andrew's church. The walls hold a few prints and a collection of old Guinness advertisements, whilst the beams and many other surfaces are crowded with the pump-clips of the countless guest beers stocked by the licensees over the past few years.

The old pele tower at Dacre Castle

Seating is largely on wall benches and settles with a few stools making the most of the limited area available. Adjoining this main room is a light, airy restaurant area created from the adjoining cottage and useful as an overspill to the popular bar. The home cooked food is both extensive in choice and excellent in quality, with ever-changing specials.

The regular beers are draught Bass and Worthington Bitter. The collection of pump-clips evidences the range of guest beers sourced during the year. More often than not there are two guests per week during the summer months and one during the winter. The hours of opening also vary throughout the year. In general between March and October the pub is open (Sunday to Friday) between 12 noon and 3pm and 5.30pm (ish) to 11pm, plus all day Saturdays. In winter (end of October to beginning of March), lunchtime opening is only at weekends between 12 noon and 3pm, with evening opening at 6pm every day. Food is available, when open, between noon and 2pm and 6pm to 9pm. In other words, if you're aiming for a lunchtime stop here en-route, then ring before leaving Pooley Bridge to check on opening, particularly in the winter!

The Walk

I've chosen to start this walk in Pooley Bridge rather than at Dacre as the parking at the Horse & Farrier is limited. This has the advantage of a welcome refreshment stop well into the walk or, on winter week-

*days, the chance of a drink at one of Pooley Bridge's pubs which tend
to be open at lunchtimes, unlike the Horse & Farrier (see the opening
hours detailed above).*

Immediately to the left of the entrance to Dunmallard Car Park is a
signpost pointing the way left along a permissive footpath for
Waterfoot. Take this, which rises gradually through the trees above the
busy road, reaching in about 400 yards a fork in the path. Bear left here,
remaining on the Waterfoot path. Losing a little height the path again
forks; here bear right to rise to a gate through the woodland edge fence.
Trace this path along to the road junction and carefully cross this. A few
paces beyond the large beech tree just beyond the junction is a waymark
post in the field. Take the path indicated for Waterfoot Caravan Site
from here, crossing the pastures and aiming for the white-painted cottages visible within the trees in the middle distance.

Waymark arrows attached to posts and gates guide you through the
edge of the permanent caravan park here to reach the front of the impressive Georgian facade of Waterfoot Farm. Carry on up the rough
drive from here, within 200 yards coming to a T-junction. The eventual
route of the walk is right, along the tarred lane. It is an interesting diversion, however, to take the concessionary footpath signposted opposite
the junction here and walk the half-mile to the ramparts of the small hill
fort of Maiden Castle. The route is waymarked; once you've reached the
Castle simply turn back to return to this junction and join the tarred
lane. The lane is quiet but for the occasional car accessing the caravan
site or farm vehicles belonging to the handful of farms which make up
the scattered settlement of Soulby. At the junction turn left and follow
this equally quiet lane the mile distance to Dacre.

The village has much of interest besides the Horse & Farrier, which
stands at the far end of the settlement. Dacre is said to be the place
where the Saxon King Athelstan met with the Scots King Constantine,
King Hywel of Cymru, King Owen of Gwent and Prince Ealdred of
Northumbria in the year 926 or 927 to sign a short-lived peace treaty.
Several centuries earlier, according to the Venerable Bede, there was a
monastery hereabouts, possibly on the site now occupied by the village
church. St Andrews Church has suffered some restoration but retains
many of its Norman features. It also boasts a very old lock; the date 1671
and initials "AP" are stamped on it, standing for Anne of Pembroke,
better known as Lady Anne Clifford, an influential landowner and
power-broker in the Northwest of England in the seventeenth century.

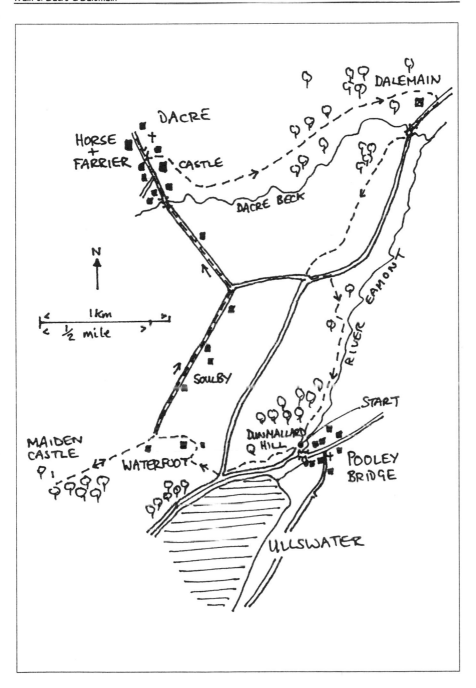

She, it seems, feared for the security of this place of worship. Its other treasures include an effigy of a crusader and remains of Saxon crosses.

It is in the churchyard, however, that other oddities are to be found. There's the vast stone slab, supported on rather thin, uneven legs alongside the path to the church door. No inscription or memorial, just a tiny sundial mounted in this desert of sandstone. Then there's the unusual triangular headstone/memorial to the Wauchope family. Most famous, however, are the four stone bears in the graveyard. Now very eroded, they purport to tell the tale of a bear waking from slumber to devour a lynx which had leaped onto its back. One theory is that they once decorated the battlements of nearby Dacre Castle. A local guidebook, available in the pub or the church, will fill in the details of these unique sculptures and other features of the village.

To leave Dacre walk downhill from the pub for about 150 yards to the old barn on the left, identified by the post-box mounted into the wall and the nearby red telephone box. Immediately past this barn go through the gate and walk ahead along the field road in front of the semi-detached houses. Round the corner and the solid old Dacre Castle is revealed. It is a pele tower, one of a comprehensive system of such fortified structures built across the northern counties of England in the 1300s to help defend the north against the marauding Scots; locally there are others at nearby Hutton John and Clifton, near Penrith. Dacre's pele is still a private residence, having been rescued several times in past centuries from near-dereliction. The austere, high stone walls, battlements and tiny-paned, leaded glass windows present a memorable sight, the walk passes right by.

For well over a mile this rough road traces a route alongside the pastures bordering Dacre Beck; look out for fallow deer, you'll certainly see umpteen pheasant and you may even glimpse one of the red squirrels which still survive hereabouts. The land is part of the estate of Dalemain, the roof and flagpole of which you'll soon be able to pick out in the gap in the wooded ridge ahead cut by the River Eamont. This great country house, Georgian on Tudor foundations and disguising medieval features, is where the rough road leads to. As you enter the courtyard look to the left for an archway, pass beneath this and walk ahead to the car park. The route is now down the driveway to the main road.

Dalemain itself is one of the premier country houses of Lakeland. Home to the Hasell family since 1679 it has renowned gardens and featured prominently in the popular television adaptation of "Jane Eyre." It's generally open to visitors from early April to early October, daily except for Fridays and Saturdays.

On reaching the main A592 turn right and follow this often busy road for about 300 yards to cross the bridge over Dacre Beck. Immediately beyond this look on the right for steps into the field and a waymark post. Head half-left across the large pasture, aiming for the far top corner at the end of the ridgetop woods. Climb the stile beside the gate here and trace the path alongside the woodland. As this curves away to the right look ahead-left for a waymark arrow pointing to another field gate, beyond which another stile beckons, virtually in line with the distant wooded hill of Dunmallard. A distinct field edge path ahead gradually falls down to a stile beside a short section of stone walling, from where walk across to the stone steps beside the road junction.

Turn left along the main road, cross to the wide verge and look for the footpath immediately before the chevron road sign. A series of plank footbridges takes the path to and alongside a line of poplars sheltering fishing ponds. Climb the stile at the far end of the poplars and trace the path to the right of the pond, entering the pasture to your right via a kissing gate. From this point onwards, simply remain with the secluded riverside path, eventually entering the woods on Dunmallard via a bridle gate. This woodland track leads directly into the car park beside the bridge at Pooley Bridge.

Walk 9. Kirksanton & Great Knott

Route: Kirksanton—Great Knott—Pohouse Lane—Whicham—Silecroft

Terrain: One climb, otherwise easy walking

Distance: 4 miles

Start: Kirksanton Village Green, roadside parking

Map: O.S. Outdoor Leisure sheet "The English Lakes, (SW)"

Access: Kirksanton is on the A5093 road about 2 miles west of Millom

Public transport: The railway station at Silecroft is on the Cumbrian Coast line; daily service except Sundays.

King William IV Inn, Kirksanton (01229 772009)

Set above the village green, the solid, three-storey King is about 200 years old and once served as the brewery tap for the nearby Bank Springs Brewery; there's a frame full of old bottle labels from this brewery, closed in the 1950s, on a wall near the bar and some old (empty...) bottles are kept at the pub. Today's beers are bang up to date and from sources nation-wide. The regular offerings at this free house are Jennings Cumberland and Best Bitter. It is the range of guest beers that make the pub worth seeking out, however. There's usually one if not two available at any one time. Whilst some are from the small independent and micro breweries which currently thrive in Cumbria, others are from much further afield. Landlord Roger Singleton resorts to inventive methods to ensure that his beers are both fresh and unusual for the area – if one of his B&B guests (four letting rooms available) is coming from afar it's been known for Roger to arrange for them to bring up a 9 gallon barrel of a local brewery's product to be made available at the King William!

The pub itself stands at the junction of the A5093 – itself a quiet country road – and the village's one lane. The capacious bar is divided into distinct sections, the heavy slated floor setting off the low beams and dark-wood settles which dot both the main bar area and the sepa-

Giant's Grave standing stones frame the old Bank Springs brewery

rate games area. Games don't include one-arm-bandits, there are none
in the pub, nor is there any piped music or juke box (or should that be
CD Selector these days...?). Decorating the walls are fascinating old
photos of this relatively little-visited area of old Cumberland, together
with water-colours and oils-on-glass painted by a talented local artist.
There are also a good number of local and regional CAMRA awards on
display, testimony to the quality of the ales and atmosphere of the King
William. Opening hours are 12noon-3pm and 7pm-11pm every day
(10.30pm Sundays), a wide choice of freshly prepared and cooked food
is available all these hours – besides being in the CAMRA Good Beer
Guide, it's also in the Good Food Guide. And a final aside – the landlord
also works at the nearby Haverigg Prison, so talk of the clink of glasses
or of lock-ins will be treated the disdain they richly deserve!

The Walk

In keeping with its name, Kirksanton village itself has no church. Local
legend has it that the old church sank into Kirksanton Moss centuries
ago, hence the name – Kirk Santon, sunken church. The immense village green is the heart of the village, its few old cottages, grand houses

and farms circling this or lying beside the back lane which peters out in the nearby burrows (sand-dunes). In many ways the village was a company town, with many of the buildings owned by the three Brocklebank brothers or vested in their Bank Springs Brewery. Near to the King William are the old excise office and stables for the brewery drays. The brewery itself, which still stands (as a private house), closed in the 1950s when it was sold to the regional brewers Matthew Brown, along with its 20 or so pub estate, stretching from Millom to Egremont.

Walk directly away from the front of the pub and south along the main road for about 150 yards to the footpath on the left signposted for Po House. Walk along this rough lane, cross the level crossing and bear right this side of the cottage, commencing a steady climb up alongside the old cart track, itself an overgrown, boggy flush up the hillside. Looking uphill you'll see a ladder stile over the high wall across the field top. Cross this and circle to the right around the area of thick gorse bushes. Your eventual target is the barn and ruined farm on the ridgetop ahead next to the small aerial; reach this via the left-hand of the two gateways at the top end of this field, then the gateway at the top-right hand corner of the next.

The farm here near the top of Great Knott is long-abandoned, though the barn is newly roofed and used as a cattle shelter. The route is waymarked through the farmyard, veering left to trace an old field road passing close to the aerial. In the pastures to the right of the ruined house is a remarkable collection of stone circles and avenues known collectively as the Lacra Circles, one of the major, if unsung, sites in the north of England. Two of the circles are fairly easily discernible, each with half a dozen or so stones still standing proud of the sheep-cropped grass, the stones of the others are toppled and half-buried, missing or difficult to pick out with an untrained eye.

Join the stony field road out of the farmyard and simply remain with it around the contour, eventually commencing a long, gentle descent. On the clearest of days the Isle of Man can be seen far out to the west, to the south the great expanse of the Duddon Sands, Walney Island, the shipyards at Barrow and, in the distance, good old Blackpool Tower. Near to hand the sea may be dotted with the small fishing boats and yachts out from Haverigg or Ravenglass or the larger vessels – even submarines – from the yards at Barrow. On the flat meadowland below there is one distinctive square stand of trees with a bare grassed area in the middle. This is said to be the spot chosen by one of the Brocklebank

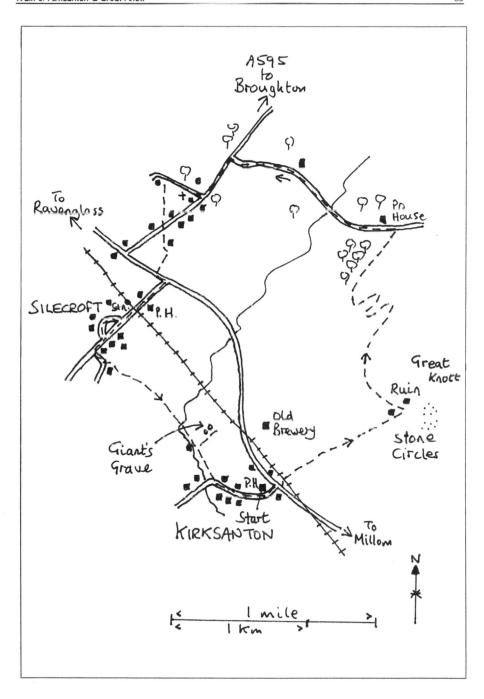

brothers on which to build a marital home. Sadly for him, the marriage never occurred and whilst the trees were planted, the house was never started.

As the track bends to the right, delightful views unfold up along the verdant Whicham Valley, sheltering at the foot of the steep slopes of Black Combe, a mass of slate rock all but isolated from the rest of the Lake District and said by some to cover the greatest area of any single mountain in England. Passing through a gate marked by an old tin bath (what an excellent business the supply of old tin baths and pot sinks must be to be involved in, you're almost guaranteed to find one or other such appliance being used as a drinking trough in isolated fields and upland pastures throughout Britain) the track steepens into a series of hairpin bends, then runs alongside a wood to a junction with a tarred lane at Po House.

Turn left along the lane and follow it the half-mile to the junction with the A595, turning left along this. As the main road in the south-western Lake District this can be a busy road. Fortunately, you've only got to run the gauntlet for about 300 yards and the sight-lines are good. There is no verge, so warily walk the 300 yards to the lane on the right (about 50 yards beyond the rough farm drive) and turn along this, soon passing by the old Whicham School House and the tiny St Mary's church. Cross the brook and rise with the narrow lane beyond. Just before reaching the house on the left at the corner, look carefully on the left for a well hidden stile – it's right at the end of the hedge. Once over this cut diagonally across the pasture to a further, double stile at the offset corner, beyond which continue down to the opposite-bottom corner to a gate and the main A595 again. Carefully cross straight over here and go along the rough lane opposite. To the right of the barn and cottage at the end is a small gate into the field, then a footbridge over a brook. Cross the field to the gate just beside the electricity pylon. Turn left, cross the road and take the lane beside the village green and war memorial which leads into Silecroft.

Entering Silecroft, the village pub, the Miners Arms (Theakstons Bitter) is passed on your left immediately before the level crossing. It's another one-street village, with a bye-lane circling past the tiny old manor house and the remains of a horse-ginn. Follow the road towards the sea to reach the speed de-restriction signs. Here on the left is a lane signposted for Southfield. Walk along this for about 50 paces to the bend, here forking left along the grassy track to the left of the white-painted bungalow, Blairgowrie. Remain with this high-hedged old field road to its end, passing by veritable banks of the orange flowered montbretia plant along the way. Cross the stile at the end and continue to the next one, visible in line with the distant farmhouse. The path is indistinct and may be a little boggy in places.

Join the line of the ditch-like brook to reach and cross the narrow footbridge, then continue towards the farm. The path keeps outside the fence to the left of the farm to reach the end of an old fieldside road near to a gate and stile. The way is over the stile, but first divert to the left and walk to the standing stones. These two stones are known as the Giant's Grave, though no burial has been excavated at the site. The larger stone does have a small cup mark cut into it. Their age is unknown, but are thought to be connected to the Neolithic stone circles and avenues found on Great Knott (Lacra) passed by earlier in this walk. From this point is a good view to the old Bank Springs Brewery, its somewhat Gothic tower nestling beneath the steep hill behind. Return to the stile, cross it and turn left along the drive. At the end continue ahead-left to return to the village green and the King William 1V.

Walk 10. Swinside's Stones

Route: The Green – Hallthwaites – Sunkenkirk – Knottend

Terrain: Field paths and farm roads, boggy in places

Distance: 5½ miles

Start: The Green; ample parking

Map: O.S. Outdoor Leisure sheet "The English Lakes, (SW)"

Access: The Green is on the A5093 immediately south of its junction with the A595, about 5 miles SW of Broughton in Furness.

The Punch Bowl Inn (01229 772605)

The green at The Green is a small triangle of grass planted with a single tree. The Punch Bowl stands opposite this, backing onto a much larger area of greensward which was, together with pastures beyond the main road, used by drovers to pasture their animals en route to the markets and ports at Millom or distant Ulverston. The Punch Bowl was thus an important stop for such travellers. There is a very difficult to read datestone above one of the doors which suggests it was standing in 1674, so the building has a long pedigree. Within, the floor is laid with the biggest stone slabs you're likely to see anywhere outside of a quarry. The large bar area is divided into distinct areas for games, dining, sitting or warming at the fire; there's also a totally separate restaurant room and a function room used regularly for music and other entertainment. Beside the usual brasses and prints, the walls host a large number of mirrors and a collection of Victorian and Edwardian photographs, both of the pub and various family/group portraits, with a few more modern additions – the snap of the rear view of three sheep and six cloth-capped farmers is sure to get a conversation going!

It's a free house, with various Jennings beers as the regulars plus an occasional guest beer. There's also an extensive menu for bar snacks and restaurant meals. Opening hours are 12 noon-2pm and 6pm-11pm (Sunday evenings 7pm-10.30pm). There's a very large car park, plus parking in the village hall car park opposite.

The Walk

Walk past the lone tree on the green and over the bridge across the Black Beck. Turn left along the quiet back lane and follow this for well over half a mile to the junction at another bridge beside cottages. Don't cross this, but take the footpath immediately beside it signposted for Thwaites Mill and trace this above the beck. As the enclosed path ends at a squeeze stile, join the line of wall on your right and continue northwards to a gate beneath a small oak, the path beyond soon developing as a walled track along the edge of the old Fox's Wood. At the far end is a choice of routes beyond the stile, favour the one which goes ahead, past the pylon and alongside a tumble-down wall on your left. Several gates bring you to a muddy lane within trees above the beck, then a short tarred section ending at the main A595 road.

Go straight across and into the line of the old road, now all-but a lay-by. Ahead is the mill referred to on the earlier footpath sign, a saw-mill. You, however, should turn right along the old road and rise with it the 250 yards to the driveway on the left leading to Beck Bank Farm. Walk in front of the farmhouse then bear left past the side, falling to a long rake of stepping stones across Black Beck. From the far bank a field

The awesome stone circle at Swinside

road leads to a gateway in a wall, pass through this and walk up to the house at the top of the steep pasture, a squeeze stile here giving access to a lane. Turn right and continue with the lane to and through a small wood. A short distance beyond this is a fork just before Cragg Hall. Here, take the rougher, left road, signposted as a bridleway to Swinside and Thwaites Fell. This continues to rise along the eastern flank of Knott Hill through superb countryside, the high fells to the left, rather more crinkly hilltops above distant Dunnerdale to the right whilst ahead rise the rounded tops of the Buck Barrow hills.

This stony road leads directly to Swinside Farm, reaching the stone circle also known as Sunkenkirk immediately beforehand, the destination of this walk. This magnificent ancient monument is as undervisited as the much more famous circle at Castlerigg, near Keswick, is popular, entirely due to the lack of roads anywhere near the site. It is thus quiet, peaceful and serene, all you need is a bright sunny day to complete the timeless scene. There are 52 stones in the monument, almost all of which still standing to form a circle some 30 yards in diameter. In your minds eye remove the nearby farm and the stone walls to appreciate the extraordinary site, close below the crags of Swinside Fell at the mouth of the deep, sombre valley between this and a limb of White Combe, at the same time overlooking extraordinary vistas to the high peaks of the central Lake District and down to the sands of the Duddon Estuary. Presumably constructed as some kind of sacred site in Neolithic times – burnt bones have been excavated at the site – the legend is that the stones were built as a church by day, only to be caused to sink into the ground at night by Old Nick, hence the alternative name of Sunkenkirk.

Return to the gate in the wall just past the cattle grid. As the roadway you arrived along bends to the left, walk straight ahead into the rough grass, heading in line of sight for the break of slope on the right of Knott Hill. A long, gradual climb across this occasionally boggy moorland (there's at least one ditch to leap across) brings you to a kissing gate close to the boundary wall corner. Walk on beyond, parallel to the wall on your right to a stile beside a gate. To the right open out views down the Whicham valley to the Irish Sea, glimpsed in the gap between the great whaleback of White and Black Combes and the lower knolls of Millom Park and Great Knott. A field track develops, leading to another field gate and views south across the wide Duddon estuary to the pla-

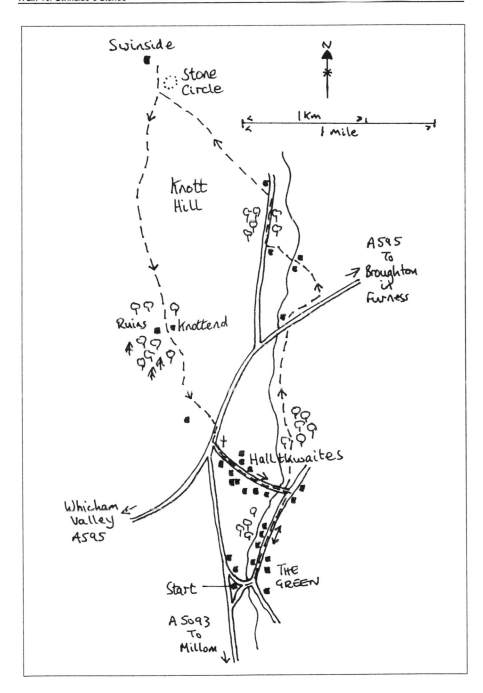

teau-like hills on the Furness Peninsula, whilst the low lying Walney Island curves away to the obvious submarine "pens" at Barrow.

Once through this gate drop to the wall at the foot of the rough, boggy pasture and trace this to the top of a walled old lane just beyond a couple of ash trees. This potentially rather wet, stony lane leads down to the tumbled remains of a farm and barns at Knottend, a rather melancholy site darkened by the immense sycamores and beech trees, an odd fruit tree and the dark ranks of a fir plantation close to hand, the whole bisected by a braided stream. The way out is through the gate and along the walled track which eventually gives out into open cow pastures. Keep a wall on your right, a waymark arrow soon confirming the route ahead to a gate and another short section of walled greenway. From the end of this head across the pasture to the gateway in line with the distant church, continuing on much the same line across the next field to the stile and gate in the corner (the end of a rough farm driveway) and the main road.

Turn right along the road, a busy stretch but with good sight-lines. Carefully cross to the church, being St James' Church at Hallthwaites, and turn sharp left immediately past the churchyard along the minor road for Hallthwaites. This drops initially steeply then levels out to wind through this delightful little hamlet to reach the bridge over Black Beck. Cross this and turn right to walk the long half-mile back to the bridge at The Green, just across which is The Punch Bowl Inn.

Walk 11. Four Stones Hill

Route: Bampton Grange — Drybarrows — Four Stones Hill — The Forces Waterfalls

Terrain: Easy walking, some scrambling, some boggy moorland patches

Distance: 6½ miles

Start: The Crown & Mitre Inn, Bampton Grange

Map: O.S. Outdoor Leisure sheet "The English Lakes, (NE)"

Access: Bampton Grange is a hamlet on unclassified roads about 7 miles south of Penrith. Follow the signs for Haweswater from the B5320 at Yanwath, just south of Penrith. Alternatively, approach from Shap on the A6, Bampton (and Shap Abbey) is signposted from the north end of the village. Bampton Grange is half-a-mile from Bampton.

Public transport: An infrequent weekend and Bank Holiday bus runs, May to September, between Penrith and Haweswater via Bampton and Bampton Grange.

The Crown & Mitre (01931 713225)

An imposing building on Bampton Grange's one street, this former coaching inn dates from late Georgian times. A porticoed entrance, topped with a wrought iron balcony, leads into the one large room served by a corner bar, with Castle Eden and Boddingtons being the fare on offer. The place to be on a winter's day is in the adjacent corner, warmed by an open fire and looking out of the deep-set window over the gaggle of cottages clustered behind the pub. The main room itself is high-ceilinged, the walls adorned with photographs of the Inn a century or so ago and a selection of paintings of the locality. The dart board and trophies are testimony both to the prowess of the throwers and the success of the pub as a local in this sparsely populated area. There's also a separate pool room, popular with field trip students and Duke of Edinburgh award seekers, both of which groups enliven evenings at this convivial local.

The Crown & Mitre retains its function as an Inn, with six letting bedrooms and B&B available year-round. As a rambler you'll be in good company; it's a popular stopping off point on the Coast to Coast walk and the originator of the new alternative Coast to Coast walk stayed here during the course of research. Bar meals are available between 12 noon and 1.30pm and 7pm to 9pm, whilst the very welcoming and sociable landlady may rustle up a sandwich at most hours. The pub is open all day every day (12 noon to 11pm, 10.30pm Sundays) except on Wednesdays when opening time is 5pm.

The Walk

Right opposite the Crown & Mitre is the village church, St Patrick's, its weathervane dating the rebuilding of the church to 1726. Surprisingly little seems known about the history of the site before this; elements of earlier days survive in the shape of an old pulpit and parish chest, but the Georgian building itself is rather austere, the bare grey-stone walls dotted with just a few memorials, mostly to the Noble family. The very name of the hamlet, Bampton Grange, suggests a long religious history. A grange was an outlying, or "Daughter" settlement of an abbey or monastery, functioning as a farm; it's likely that the monks of Shap Abbey, just a few miles up the Lowther valley, established the site in the 1400s.

Walk down to the bridge over the Lowther (turn right from the pub's front door), cross it and bear left along the road signed for Mardale and Haweswater. Within a few paces look on the right for the prominent ladder stile your side of the solid, but rarely used or served bus shelter. Climb this and trace the wall on your right to another large stile, from which continue across the field to the stile beside the chapel at the far side. Walk to the lane and turn right, crossing the bridge over Haweswater Beck to reach a crossroads. Go straight across and up along the "Dead End" lane, following this gradually uphill for a good half-mile. Pass by the driveway signposted for Littlewater (left), then within a few paces look on the left for a public footpath sign just beyond a wall. From the stile here the secluded Littlewater Tarn can be seen nestling in a hollow in these low fells, the craggy tops of Swindale Common providing a dappled backdrop.

Draw a course to bisect the pasture to the right, aiming for a ladder stile roughly in line with the distant stone barn. Climb a further ladder stile in the far-left corner of the next smaller field, from which it is easy

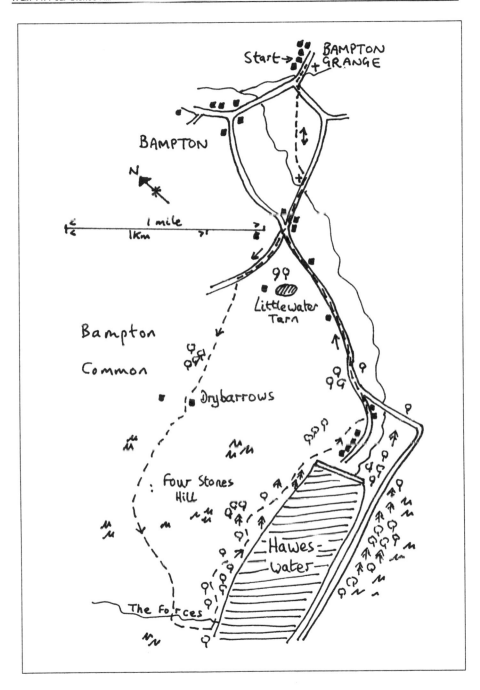

Start→ BAMPTON GRANGE

BAMPTON

N

1 mile
1km

Littlewater Tarn

Bampton Common

Drybarrows

Four Stones Hill

Hawes Water

The Forces

to spot the next two stiles, one within a few yards, the other some yards to the left of the barn at the top of the field. This latter stile is particularly high (all of seven steps), beyond it bear left to the wall beside the electricity pole, then pass through the field gate 50 or so yards below and walk to the cottage at the head of the rough field. Walk along the rough drive, keeping the cottage on your left, then pass through gates to the left of the barn. This is a concessionary path. Through the second gate keep right alongside the trees for about 25 yards, then as the wall bends away to the right continue slightly right and gradually uphill through the bracken. Within 150 yards or so you'll pick up an obvious rough field road (the farm of Drybarrows is down to your right), follow this through the dip in the low ridge and walk to the boggy area about 200 yards further along the field road. Ford the brook here and pick up the wide green path which cuts a swathe through the bracken (N.B. not the narrower, steeper one off to the right). This rises gradually from the flat, boggy floor of the shallow valley.

Continue the gradual climb for about 500 yards, at which point the green path forks. Take the left fork, a sometimes stony and boggy path which brings you in about 500 yards to a great pile of stones and a small circular structure in a shallow pass beneath a rocky crag. This has been identified as a prehistoric cairn; more instantly recognisable ancient artefacts stand on the hillside about 100 yards beyond the shallow pond the path now passes to the left of. The two low standing stones are only half the story, the other two, long since vanished, gave the hill its prosaic name. Maybe one reason for siting the stones here on Four Stones Hill was the spectacular view which opens out up to the head of Mardale, encircled by a clutch of "Two Thousand Footers" – Artlecrag Pike, Harter Fell and Mardale Ill Bell. In the 1930s the leafy seclusion of Mardale village and Mardale Tarn were destroyed to allow the creation of Haweswater, the reservoir now filling the deep valley. Twice since the mid-1970s, the water level has dropped to such an extent that the packhorse bridge, old field roads and walls of the drowned village, near to the top end of the valley, have been visible.

The reservoir was created at the behest of Manchester Corporation, water still flows to there and to other northern towns along the way. The villagers of Mardale were resettled, the traditional annual shepherd's meet, held for centuries at the Dun Bull Inn, is now held at Bampton. The old church was demolished, those buried in the graveyard were dis-interred to be re-buried at a church in Shap. The final service was held at the old church on 18th August 1935 and attended by enormous crowds (some figures of over 2000 have been suggested). The service was conducted not by the long-incumbent vicar, F.H.J. Barham, but by the Bishop of Carlisle. Such are the trappings of high office. The only buildings in the upper valley nowadays are the valve tower and pier reaching out into the lake and the isolated Haweswater Hotel, the large, rather sombre looking building visible in the trees on the far (east) bank of the water.

With the standing stones on your left, head half right to rejoin the grassy track which now drops very gradually around the hillside (*N.B.*

Haweswater from The Forces waterfalls

make sure you don't take the narrower path which heads almost directly downhill towards the reservoir). In places it is boggy underfoot, in others fairly indistinct amidst the bracken. A stirring view up the rather forbidding Fordingdale Bottom, carved by the Measand Beck into the heights of Bampton Common and the long ridge of High Street, opens out to your right, a sure sign that you're on the right track. The ever-present sheep graze the fellsides, here joined by semi-wild fell ponies, an increasingly rare sight.

Soaring high above, that large bird of prey may just be a Golden Eagle; one of the inaccessible crags towards the head of Haweswater is the sole nesting site in England of these once common hunters. The long, easy descent reaches Measand Beck at a sturdy footbridge.

Cross the bridge, turn left and pick a way down alongside or above the water. This is a delightful section of the walk, Measand Beck tumbling over a long series of torrents, shoots and falls known collectively as "The Forces". The narrow gorge deepens as it falls towards the lake, the sides festooned with mosses and great hanging tresses of heather whilst red-berried rowan trees, small birch and oak somehow maintain a foothold.

At the foot of the falls cross the concrete tractor bridge and join the rough lakeside road, water off to your right beyond some small surviving hay meadows. The way now is simply to remain with this stony road for nearly two miles, its undulating course passing through stands of fragrant pines. The lakeside woods are thin enough to allow views across to the far bank, impressive steep crags clothed in old oakwoods tumbling virtually straight into the reservoir. On a sunny summer day it's pleasant to take time out for a few minutes to appreciate the array of wild birds which share the valley with you; if you're particularly observant and lucky you may also see small lizards darting about amidst the roadside wall-stones. Red squirrels live in the woods whilst the increasingly rare crossbill has been recorded feeding in the uppermost branches of the spruces during the winter months, attracted here from the vast forests of Russia and Scandinavia by the warmer climate.

The rough road passes well above the dam (90 feet high, 1150 feet long and holding back 18,600 million gallons when the reservoir is full) and eventually reaches a gate and stile leading through the trees and to the reservoir access road and treatment works. Turn left along the tarred road. Alternatively, it is common local practice to remain in the pasture, following the wide green path through the bracken, favouring the lower way at any fork to reach the roadway at a field gate well beyond the treatment plant. Turn left along the same tarred access road and keep left at any junction to reach a crossroads and cottages nearly a mile distant. Turn right to the chapel beyond the bridge over Haweswater Beck, climb the stile just along the driveway here and re-trace the initial part of the walk to return to Bampton Grange, visible across the pastures.

Walk 12. Shap Abbey and The Lowther Valley

Route: Shap — Shap Abbey — Ralfland Forest — Keld

Terrain: Easy walking on field paths and back lanes

Distance: 4½ miles

Start: Shap. Large car park beside the Crown Inn

Map: O.S. Outdoor Leisure sheet "The English Lakes (NE)"

Access: The small town of Shap is on the A6 between Kendal and Penrith (somewhat nearer the latter). It is also signposted off the M6 motorway, Junction 39 (2 miles).

The Crown Inn (01931 716229)

This small, white painted building is obviously much older than the commercial offices onto which it is tacked, probably a couple of centuries old at least going by some of the beams visible within. A corner bar serves a large L-shaped room, the older part of the building at the front, a more modern extension behind (and with plans for further extension to provide a restaurant area). A wide variety of prints and brasses stud the wall, shelves and alcoves, wall benches provide much of the seating.

The Crown's owners go out of their way to make walkers welcome. More than a few "Coast to Coast" walkers pop in as it's on the route – the bunk house out back is a handy place to overnight, camping in the pub garden is also encouraged whilst the pampered "C2C-er" can take advantage of B&B. Opening hours can also be useful to the casual walker. Whilst the posted hours are just 7pm-11pm on Mondays to Thursdays, if you're in Shap during licensing hours (i.e. from 11am), a ring on the front door bell will usually effect entry to the pub! On Fridays to Sundays the opening hours are 12 noon-11pm (10.30pm Sundays).

Despite the collection of old brass beer-taps behind the bar, the "Traditional Ale" advertised on the board outside is cooled, elec-

tric-pumped Theakston's Bitter, the font nestling amongst smoothflow
dispensers for John Smiths and Worthington amidst other lager pumps.
The bar cries out for a handpump or two! This aside, the pub is a genu-
inely welcoming stop – and who knows, if enough people ask for the real
thing then hand pulled draught beer may once again flow at The Crown
Inn in Shap.

Shap Abbey

The Walk

Bear left from the front door, almost immediately passing by the old Market Hall, a fascinating little building dating from the seventeenth century, now housing the town's library. (Shap's main street is fronted by many centuries-old cottages and larger houses, a fine half-timbered old manor is about 200 yards to the north). Almost opposite, behind old cottages and up a lane rising gently to the limestone hills to the east, is the old market town's parish church of St Michael. Rebuilt about 150 years ago but of Norman origin, it received the remains of those folk buried in Mardale church when this was demolished during the construction of the Haweswater Reservoir in the 1930s. Take the first turn left past the library, an un-named (November 1998) road leading to a new development of housing. In about 50 yards turn right along the narrow, rough road which runs between the foot of the gardens of the old houses lining Shap's main street and those of a newer estate to your left. Simply remain with this lane, which eventually comes to an end near to a small old stone barn. Remain on the same line, now following the grassy path between hedges and walls to eventually emerge onto a minor road at a bend. Turn left and trace the lane for about 150 yards to a double footpath signpole on your right just beyond the stone barn. Climb the stile into the field and turn left for Shap Abbey, roughly paralleling the stone field wall to reach a narrow stile at the corner. Continue through the next field along the line of wall to a gate in the corner, at a sharp road bend and junction. Directly opposite is a stile and sign for Shap Abbey. Again, walk within the field wall to the far left corner, beyond which simply follow the surfaced road steeply downhill to the car park for Shap Abbey. Cross the old stone bridge here and wind round to the Abbey itself.

The Abbey of St Mary Magdalene here at Shap was established by monks of the Premonstratensian persuasion in the early thirteenth century, though the most striking part of the ruins, the solid west tower, is much later. Its site, hidden in the deep valley of the Lowther, was probably deliberately chosen as a form of defence; from a distance, marauding raiders from Scotland would probably not see it and thus pass it, and its moveable wealth, by. This form of strategic thinking is not unknown elsewhere, St David's Cathedral in Wales is similarly built within a deep valley, protection against being seen from the ships of raiders throughout the Dark Ages and after; Furness Abbey is on a similar site. In the care of English Heritage, there is no admission charge. Information boards offer on-site interpretation of the rather scant remains of this lonely old foundation beside the banks of the Lowther.

The waters of the Lowther are put to good use immediately downstream of the old bridge, where a sheep-dipping location can be seen. Sheep were directed into the tapering walled pathway which ends above a deep pool in the river, into which they must leap to gain escape via the stony "beach" opposite. It's in remarkably good condition, I'd hazard a guess that its still in use, at least as a sheep-wash (as opposed to today's chemically based dipping).

To follow the route away from the Abbey, stand with your back to the small entrance gate (the Abbey Farm off to your left along the driveway) and retrace your steps along the green track towards the car park. This brings you to the bridge and sheep dip mentioned above. Just before reaching this look up to the left to find and cross the ladder stile beneath the gaunt old oak. Beyond the stile follow the path above the high river bank for about 100 yards then cut left across the field, rising gently along the well-walked path to find another ladder stile across the wall at the top of this long pasture. Walk across the large field beyond, heading for the point where the wall disappears over the near horizon. On reaching the line of an old wall (now just a series of humps down the slope) beneath the line of electricity cables turn left, following the line of old wall, then the extant wall, to a stile in the corner.

The line of oaks grows along the course of a prehistoric earthwork here at the edge of Ralfland Forest. It undoubtedly predates this, as the name "Forest" is a Norman term usually given to areas reserved for the hunt and the chase beloved of the Norman and Angevin kings, courtiers and acolytes. It may be several thousand years since the area actually was deforested, the peat moors and bogs which characterise Ralfland being the eventual fate of these trees of millennia past. The earthwork is just one of a vast number of standing stones, tumuli, circles, avenues and cairns dotting these upland wastes in the Shap area.

Climb the stile and bear slightly right across the boggy pasture to reach a tarred lane, turn left along this and rise gradually to a junction, here turning left. This concreted moorland road is laid on the trackbed of a railway built to expedite the construction of the Haweswater dam in the early 1930s. It ran from a junction with the main line at Shap Summit (about a mile south of the works which you can't fail to see in the middle distance), transporting the great number of enormous gran-

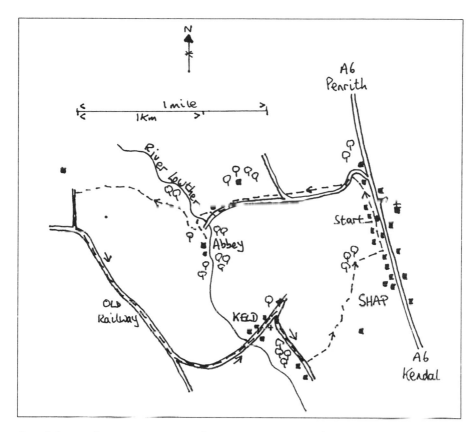

ite slabs and vast tonnages of concrete used in the construction of the dam.

Remain with this roadway for about a mile, skirting the edge of the wilderness of Ralfland Forest, to reach a junction, here bearing left to Keld. This tiny hamlet's name is derived from the Norse word for spring. It seems likely that such a spring gave rise to the settlement and that, as seems common in medieval times, holy properties were ascribed to the waters, resulting in the establishment of a shrine, then a chapel about 500 years ago. The chapel still stands, a rough built stone building, slate roofed with small windows now in the care of the National Trust. Other origins for the chapel are also convincingly made – as a Chantry or a detached chapel tied to the nearby Shap Abbey; there's no general agreement. It's kept locked, but the keys are available from a nearby cottage.

This enigma stands at the top end of the hamlet, immediately beyond which you should turn sharp right along the lane signed for Thornship. Follow this walled, wildflower-rich lane above the wooded Lowther Valley to reach the first farm buildings. On the left here climb steps to a squeeze stile through the wall and a footpath sign for Shap. In a further 100 yards pass through another squeeze stile then keep the zig-zag wall on your left, another stile leading to a gradually rising field and a walled green lane beyond the headwall. Turn left along this, then in about 100 yards climb the stone-step stile on the right. The long, straggling township of Shap is now visible in the distance, drawn out along the A6, the old high road to Scotland.

Sight the copse of trees half-left in the middle distance and walk to this via a series of gap stiles. Pass through the right-hand edge of the copse, climb the stile in the corner and follow the line of wall/fence to the right side of the modern warehouse. Immediately beyond this turn left along the rough lane, in about 50 yards reaching the back gate to the beer garden and car park of The Crown Inn.

Walk 13. The Vale of Nightshade

Route: Dalton – Furness Abbey – Newton – Standing Tarn

Terrain: Easy walking in undulating countryside

Distance: 6 miles

Start: The Brown Cow Inn, Dalton-in-Furness

Map: O.S. Outdoor Leisure sheet "The English Lakes, (SW)"

Access: Dalton is now bypassed off the A590, about 4 miles NE of Barrow-in-Furness. The Brown Cow stands at Goose Green, at the foot of the hill immediately below the church and castle. Park at the pub, or in the square beside the castle and walk down Church Street.

Public transport: Dalton railway station is on the Furness Line, daily service between Lancaster and Barrow-in-Furness. Through services operate to/from Preston and Manchester. Buses to Dalton from Barrow, Ulverston and Kendal.

The Brown Cow (01229 462553 or 468881)

Quite possibly the oldest building in Dalton after the castle and church, the pub's deeds go back to AD1500, although research suggests that the foundation may be a century or so before that. The cosy free house nestles in a secluded setting at the foot of the high bluff on which are built the castle and church, accompanied by a handful of old cottages and houses. A series of interconnected, low rooms wind to two sides of the bar, the two front rooms warmed by wood-burning stoves. Some of the great ceiling beams are rumoured to have come from Furness Abbey at the time of its dissolution. The usual selection of brasses, photographs and prints is augmented by a variety of warming pans. Sash-windows at the front look out onto a roomy terrace set with tables and benches, a veritable sun trap near to the small beck.

The regular beers are Theakston's Bitter and XB and Courage Directors, with at least one changing guest ale. The Brown Cow is open virtually all permitted hours (12 noon-11pm [10.30pm Sundays]), offers a good range of food and you can also base yourself here as a B&B guest, an ideal centre for the whole of Furness.

The Walk

Stride directly away from the pub's front door to the small car park about 100 yards distant. Turn right here with the footpath sign for Millwood and skirt the car park, soon bearing left, again at a sign for Millwood. A wide gravel path skirts the woodland edge, narrowing and becoming muddier as it leaves the company of the road above and traces a route beside and below the railway line to Barrow. Passing below a signal box, the first of several gates is encountered before the path passes beneath the railway. A further passage beneath another line follows in about 300 yards, the path then merging into a rough old lane which gradually rises to a main road.

The way now is directly opposite, but you're at a dangerous corner, so bear right for a short distance before crossing and walking back to the path, signposted as a footpath to Furness Abbey. The initially wide path soon deteriorates into a narrow way between the railway embankment and a long pasture. The narrow, wooded valley here is known as the Vale of Nightshade and here and there, in season, the thickly vegetated path is indeed hung with growths of woody nightshade (bittersweet), its purplish flowers of summer succeeded by red berries in autumn. This isn't a path for those wearing shorts as the nettles and brambles can be problematical in summer. Persevere, however, for the route passes beneath the railway to emerge onto a narrow lane, within a hundred or so yards reaching the Abbey Inn and the ruinous archway over the road.

This is the northern limit of the remarkable ruins of Furness Abbey, originally founded in AD1127 as a daughter house to the great French Abbey at Savigny. Set in the narrow, wooded valley of Bekansgill, the foundation grew to become the second wealthiest of all the Cistercian Houses in Britain. The valley site offered the seclusion sought by the monks and the advantage of being shielded from the gaze of Danish raiders and pirates who still haunted the nearby Irish Sea in the twelfth and thirteenth centuries. With their business acumen, royal patronage (King Stephen gave the land on which the abbey is built) and religious fervour the monks established agricultural, mining and iron smelting businesses which allowed them to expand their initial small-scale religious house into the massive complex, the remains of which are visible

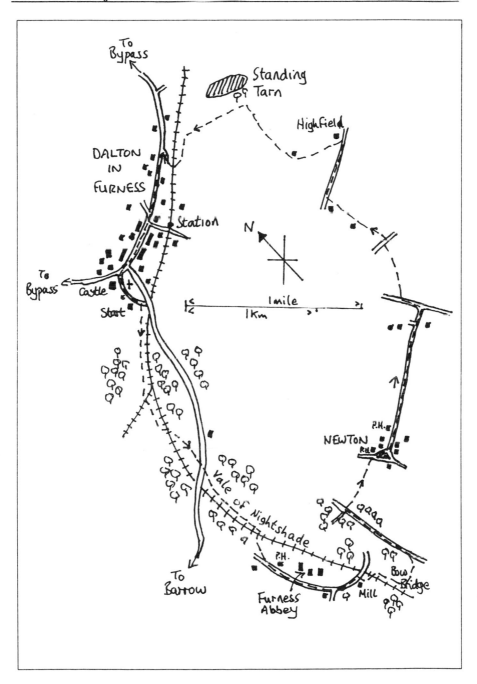

today. It would be quite easy to spend several hours here to fully appreciate the site which, not being on the "mainstream" tourist routes enjoyed by the more famous abbeys such as Fountains or Tintern, is consequently remarkably undervisited and relatively unknown. Were this site in the centre of Lakeland it would be overrun – enjoy its tranquillity! There is an admission charge, the site is open daily from April 1st to October 1st, closed on Mondays and Tuesdays the rest of the year.

The lane skirts the boundary fence of the Abbey complex, affording good views of the main buildings including the west tower and the infirmary chapel, the solid, detached building passed by close to just after you ignore the turn to the Town Centre, remaining instead with the boundary fence. On your right just as the road begins to climb is the old Abbey Mill, restored to other use by various youth employment projects. Immediately past the mill take the path on the right which becomes a railed path leading to a crossing on the level over the railway. Once across turn right and walk down the long pasture, tracing the line of the mill leat. Cross the slab bridge and continue downstream to the medieval Bow Bridge, an old packhorse bridge in a sylvan setting. Cross this, walk to the lane and turn left.

At the road junction look on your right for a footpath signposted for Newton. Beyond the kissing gate walk to the low waymarker post in the field, then climb the steep pasture to find a metal kissing gate in the top wall. Take a breather here as an excuse to take in the expansive views. Close to hand are the terraces of Barrow with the shipyards beyond and the curving bank of Walney Island. The busy shipping lane beyond takes the eye out to the several gas rig platforms tapping the resources of the Irish Sea basin. To the north the high mountains of the Coniston area rise steeply and darkly beyond the undulating limestone crags and commons of the Furness Peninsula.

Head across the fields to the village of Newton, leaving the field opposite The Village Inn. Turn right down the lane directly in front of the pub, which soon bends left to wind through this small village, passing by the other village pub, The Farmers Arms, near the far end. Simply remain with this quiet country road as it rises gradually out of Newton. The high hedges lessen here and there to allow views to the distant Lakeland hills; nearer to hand the brick chimney visible up the lane opposite North Stank Farm marks the site of one of many small iron mines which survived here until well into this century.

The lane ends at a T-junction. Turn left here and walk for about 200

Shades of times past in the Vale of Nightshade

yards to the signposted footpath on the right for Long Lane. Head for the left of the field to find a narrow squeeze stile about 30 yards down from the corner. Once through this sight the distant quarry face and, nearer to hand, the two closely-spaced pylons beyond the foot of the field. The next stile is in line with these at the bottom corner of the field, beyond this walk the few paces to a further stile and turn right along the lane. Within just a few paces take the signposted bridleway on the left, immediately in front of the village signpost for Stainton with Adgarley. This potentially muddy, high-hedged route rises gently to the farm buildings at Malkin Hall Farm, from where follow the driveway to the minor road and turn right along this.

Follow the lane down into the shallow valley and up the far side to reach the barns to Highfield Farm on your left. Look for the squeeze stile here at the end of the hedge, there's also a signpost for Standing Tarn and Dalton. From this head for the sharp field corner immediately beyond the long, low, black-stained barn. At this corner raise your eyes to the horizon ahead. If the weather is clear you'll catch a glimpse of the Isle of Man through the depression in the line of the hills ahead. From the corner walk down to the concrete sheds below-right via an awkward squeeze stile. Pass beside the sheep dip here then climb the stile to the left up the steps. The rough raised bank here is the route of an old mine railway. Follow this uphill to a stile beyond the messy infilled cutting, this stile gives access to a rough, bush infested field corner and a pond in a deep hollow. Beyond the pond (most easily passed to its right) walk down the pasture towards the little Standing Tarn now visible in the depression ahead. No great shakes by Lake District standards, it's nonetheless a peaceful setting, wading cattle often adding that picturesque, bucolic touch.

Just before you reach this, however, is a squeeze stile through the wall at your end of the line of trees on your left. Head across the pasture beyond, passing by the odd mound to the field gates. Turn right along the rough track here, then go through the gate on the left just a few steps along. Trace the field edge to the stile in the far wall, here turning left along the rough path. This leads into a surfaced lane beside cottages, keep right at the fork to pass beneath the railway and wind with the lane past the new houses to the main road. Turn left.

You're soon in the lively centre of Dalton-in-Furness. Keep left at Tudor Square (with the Black Bull Pub beside it) and then ahead along Market Street, passing by the Wellington pub to rise uphill to the old part of the town clustered around the castle. It's now no more than a four-square tower set at one end of the pleasant square of old cottages and pubs. Its history is uncertain, it may well be a pele tower built as a defence against Scottish raiders in the 1300s. In the ownership of the National Trust, it's only open on Saturday afternoons in summer. Pass to the left of the castle and walk down Church Street to return to the Brown Cow. The parish church, at the top of Church Street, is believed to stand on the site of the original hamlet, recorded in the Domesday Book as Daltune; in its graveyard is a memorial to George Romney, that most fashionable of portrait painters in the mid-eighteenth century.

Walk 14. The Villages of East Furness

Route: Little Urswick – Scales – Gleaston – Stainton

Terrain: Easy walking on field paths and back lanes

Distance: 5 miles

Start: The Swan, Little Urswick. Car park opposite.

Map: O.S. Outdoor Leisure sheet "The English Lakes, (SW)"

Access: From Ulverston take the A590 towards Barrow-in-Furness. Beyond Swarthmoor turn left at the sign for Great Urswick and continue through the village to Little Urswick. The Swan is on the right at the far end of the village.

Public transport: Infrequent weekday bus service from Ulverston, service 10.

The Swan, Little Urswick (01229 869549)

The villages of the Furness Peninsula evidence a remarkable capacity for the retention of things past when it comes to pubs. Bucking the trend found in most other country areas of England, where many a village local has gone to the wall in the past two decades, all but the smallest Furness hamlet still boasts a pub – many boast two, even though the resident village population can be counted almost on the fingers of one hand. The Swan at Little Urswick is a fine example of an uncompromising village local. No pretensions to cater for the foody set in search of the rural idyll here; maybe the odd bag of crisps or nuts – even a tube of smarties or a sticky lollipop (the Swan also acts as the tuck shop for local kids) – but otherwise the pub remains a place for drinking and village chat. The village itself is no more than a few farms and a veneer of old cottages and yeoman's houses skirting the green.

Situated at the south end of Little Urswick, the pub's beer garden is a terrace at the head of the long village green, offering pleasant views across this to the low hills of east Furness. Within, one bar serves two distinct sides of the pub, a side largely dedicated to games and a drinkers den, both pleasantly furnished, both with old beams and with deep-set windows replete with window seats. Apparently the pool room area used to be the village schoolroom – visions of a mis-spent youth or two here! The somewhat dark interior of the pub, a product of the partially bare-stone and dark wood walls, is dotted with a few tables, wall settles and mixed tables, warmed in the colder months by a crackling fire.

This pleasant, whitewashed pub is still badged as a Hartleys pub, despite the demise of this company in 1982 when it was taken over by Robinsons of Stockport and the closure of the Ulverston brewery in 1991, since when the beers have been ferried up the M6 from Cheshire. Locals still yearn for the crisp taste of the beer of old. Nonetheless, the XB is kept in exemplary fashion by the young landlady, being dispensed via unusual wooden handpumps. Opening hours are all day every day (i.e. 12 noon-11pm [10.30pm on Sundays]), ample time to enjoy the character of this welcoming old local hostelry.

Gleaston Castle and Castle Farm

The Walk

Cross the village green on the stony track which cuts across it virtually from the front door of the Swan. A footpath sign for Braithwaite Lane stands beside the bus shelter, pointing across the road and into the farmyard. Walk straight through this yard, leaving by the small red-painted metal kissing gate immediately to the right of the stone-based, corrugated sheet garage. Pass through the next gate and walk up the long, narrow pasture to the far end where a kissing gate near the left corner leads to a green lane. Turn right along this, then right again along the minor road.

In but 50 or so yards go left at the footpath sign and walk up the long field to the kissing gate in the top right-hand corner. Pass through this and trace the top end of this field, ignoring the kissing gate soon reached on your left. The end of the field is marked by a very narrow squeeze stile beside a walled up old gateway, past which simply keep the field boundary on your right. An initially overgrown green lane gradually develops, walk along this to the junction with another farm lane and turn right here. You'll eventually reach the lane serving the hamlet of Scales, turn left along this.

The main part of the hamlet lies some distance along the lane as it rises up to the low limestone scars of Scales Hagg. The walk doesn't take this route, however. About 100 yards after joining the lane look on the right for a rough road, immediately past the gateway to Low Orchard. Take this, which bends around to a couple of garages. Pass to the left of these, then turn left along the line of the tall hedge/fence and trace this almost the full length of the field. The stile out of the field is about 50 yards before the acute corner and on your left. Turn right along the lane, soon passing by the small Mere Tarn, nestling in its reedy hollow in the gentle hills.

Cresting a rise, the walk reaches surely one of Furness's most delightful scenes, the ruins of Gleaston Castle. Look at any collection of Victorian and Edwardian views of the countryside and you're sure to find a photograph of a venerable old ruined church or castle, covered in ivy and used as a cattle byre. Such scenes were swept from the face of the countryside by the Ministry of Works and their successors after the Second War – ivy removed, walls re-pointed, cattle fenced out and the surrounding pastures sanitised and mown. Thankfully this treatment simply passed Gleaston Castle by.

The fractured remains of the keep, reaching for the sky like the pinnacles of rock in Monument Valley made famous in countless western films, stand on a small mound whilst below, two surviving square towers gently crumble beneath the weight of miles of ivy. Parts of curtain walls survive beside the lane, whilst a farmhouse built in mid-Victorian times nestles between the towers. Jackdaws squabble as they swoop in and out of the red-brick, empty windows. A stream meanders past the foot whilst a mill leat strikes off to the distant village. And yes, cattle do graze amidst the ruins. It's an idyllic, bucolic scene, and one in which you can share, for the friendly farmer is pleased to allow the occasional passer by to explore the ruins – just ask at the farmhouse. The castle was built in the fourteenth century by the locally powerful Harrington family; they supported the losing side during the Wars of the Roses and consequently were dispossessed by Henry 7th. The castle looks as if it has been slowly mouldering away since then; some claim that it was never actually finished and lived in.

Passing by the farm, the lane rises above the mill leat, which suddenly disappears off the face of the earth – you try espying its course in the meadows behind the hedge! Further along the lane the destination of the leat is reached around a corner. Gleaston Cornmill is an eye-catching limestone edifice, more-so as the eighteen-foot wheel, fed by the miraculously reappeared leat, virtually hangs over the edge of the lane. The current mill dates from 1774, built on a much earlier site, long-term excavations are gradually revealing earlier history. The mill is open to visitors every day except Mondays from 11am, there's a restaurant/cafe and a craft workshop at the site.

A short distance along the lane the village of Gleaston is reached, a delightful settlement of old cottages and farms, with the occasional modern intrusion. It's the sort of place that should boast a tiny inn, but is sadly one of those rare Furness villages without a pub. At the sharp bend as you enter the village continue ahead, walking through to the crossroads at the far end. Cross straight over here, up the road towards Dendron and Dalton. Here is an oddity, the lane climbs, yet at the crest you cross a stream. Just a quirk of the local morphology. Pass the cottages and walk downhill to the bend. On the right here a bridleway sign points the way for Stainton. This gradually rises along the field edge to reach the farm at Harbarrow, isolated on its tree-dotted hilltop. Join the driveway and follow this to the junction with the minor road, bearing left along this.

The village of Stainton with Adgarley is in view long before you

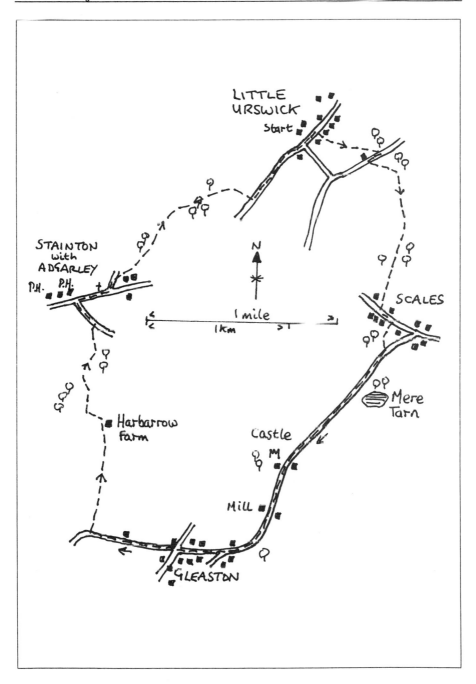

reach it, dominated by the limestone quarries behind. It's not these that catch the eye as you reach the village but, rather, the vast, craggy, boulder-strewn common that effectively acts as the village green. A strand of old cottages and a farm with an enormous chimney lie along the lane, added to in recent times by a new development. Yet this tiny village boasts two old pubs. Make the most of it!

Turn right along the road in front of the pubs (one at the junction, one off to your left), pass by the old chapel and fork left up the lane. In about 50 yards go right with the footpath sign and walk along the narrow path to the rough pasture at the end. Go straight across this, falling slightly to your right to join the muddy field lane. Persevere with this until it gives out into a field. Keep to the left side of this, rising to pass through a gate. About 30 yards up this field pass to the left side of the wall, continuing uphill to a stile in the corner. Further stiles lead into a pasture with a pond in a dip near the corner. Bear half-right across this field, passing just to the left of the right-hand outcrop of limestone and walk on to the offset corner marked by two maple trees. Round the corner, go through the gate, then pass through the left hand of the two gates just beyond. To the left of the three trees at the far side of this field is a stile onto a lane. Turn left along this to return to Little Urswick.

Walk 15. Muncaster Fell

Route: Ravenglass – Muncaster Castle – Hooker Crag – Muncaster Head – Esk Estuary

Terrain: Rough and boggy on Muncaster Fell, otherwise easy paths and farm roads

Distance: 10½ miles

Start: Ravenglass village car park (N.B. not the station car park).

Map: O.S. Outdoor Leisure sheet "The English Lakes, (SW)"

Access: Ravenglass is signposted off the A595 about 12 miles south of Egremont.

Public transport: Ravenglass station is on the Cumbrian Coast Line, with daily services (except Sundays) between Carlisle and Barrow.

The Ratty Arms (01229 717676)

The old station building of the Furness Railway's Ravenglass Station was rejuvenated in 1974 as this enterprising free house (trains still stop at the station, which is on the scenic Cumbrian Coast line). The name comes from the nickname given to the Ravenglass & Eskdale Railway (R&E), whose 15 inch gauge line commences from the station just across the tracks from the Ratty Arms (get to it via the footbridge). No surprise then that there are many prints and photographs of this little railway in the pub. There's one main room, with the bar running about half its length, and a separate, enclosed veranda looking out over the standard gauge tracks to the R&E just beyond. Outside, a capacious terrace and patio offer ample opportunity to catch the sun. Near mid-summer each year the pub is a popular stopping off point for the support crews of those brave (foolhardy?...) souls competing in the annual Three Peaks race – a challenge to climb the highest peaks in Wales (Snowdon), England (Scafell Pike) and Scotland (Ben Nevis). They travel between countries by yacht, Ravenglass is the most convenient mooring for the Scafell stage.

Ravenglass Harbour

As a free house the beer range will vary. There are 5 handpumps, Jennings' Bitter and Cumberland ales and Theakston's Bitter appear to be the regular brews, with a guest often from a local micro brewery. The extensive collection of "Good Beer Guide" stickers on a window at the entrance is proof enough of the beer's quality over the years. A good range of bar meals is available, including salads and sandwiches made with locally caught crab in season. Opening hours vary between summer and winter. In summer (May to September) it's 11am-11pm (12 noon-10.30pm Sundays), the rest of the year the bar is closed between 3pm and 6pm (7pm Sundays), except Saturdays when all day is still the rule. Got that?

The Walk

*You can cut this walk's length virtually in half by returning on the R&E from Irton Road Station. If you plan to do this, don't fail to pick up a timetable leaflet (there's usually a stock at the pub) **now** to ensure the trains are running – they do so for the majority of the year.*

Ravenglass was the most important port in the North-West in Roman times. Called *Glannaventa*, it was defended by a garrison of 1000 men, at least some of whom will have used the facilities of the Bath House known today as Walls Castle, passed near the end of the walk. Nothing else remains of the occupation, and today's population is dramatically less than in those far off days. From medieval times until the 1800s there remained a flourishing tidal port, but this trade was largely killed off by the railway, leaving the old market town's influence to decline to the pleasant village of today. The village's one street is the start of the walk, simply stroll from the car park to the promenade and turn left. The street, lined by an eclectic array of cottages, villas, town houses, former inns and workshops, peters out at the estuaryside.

(At the highest of tides this next short section is untenable. In this case return to the large public car park. From the back of the car park cross the footbridge (the R&E station is down to the left) and walk along the footpath to the end. Turn right along the lane, signed as the way to Walls Castle/Roman Bath House. Pass by the caravan site, then the ruins, and continue to the junction with a lane off to the left, marked by a waymark arrow and defined by the very tall pine).

Turn left along the foreshore and walk across the shingle and ooze for about a quarter of a mile. It's not as unpleasant as it sounds, there are plenty of wading birds to take the interest (oystercatchers, knot, etc.), the strand line may offer up much beside uprooted seaweed and the activities of yachts, small launches and fishing smacks are a diversion. Ignore the first waymark post you reach and remain on the shingle, following the blue arrow. You'll reach a further waymark post sunk into the shingle above the high tide mark. Bear left off the foreshore here and pass beneath the railway, then turn left along the rough lane and walk with it to and past the vast Edwardian mansion of Walls. Around 100 or so yards past this is a junction. Turn right here with the waymark, there's also a very tall pine and a number of shorter ones here.

Walk up this lane, lined by magnificent old trees, passing by a waymarked route to the left. Immediately before you reach the pebbledashed farm of Newtown on your right, look left for the signposted public footpath. This climbs gradually up through the fir plantation, ignoring any side paths to left and right brings you to the headwall of the woods. Once in the open field beyond aim to pass immediately to the left of the knoll, then look half-right to the long high wall enclosing the woods. There's a stile and gate through this wall, once over which follow the well defined path down into the estate surrounding Muncaster Castle. These woods are dotted with ornamental trees as well as native varieties, the path is lined with growths of Chinese Cane. It's a picturesque approach to the gardens surrounding the Castle, the ancestral home of the Pennington family. Leaving the trees, head across the lawn to pass to the left of the entrance to the Stable Yard, here joining a drive which rises from the Castle's ancillary buildings and past the medieval St Michael's Chapel to the main road. This is all too brief a visit to the attractions here at Muncaster Castle, make time if you can to return and visit at leisure this fascinating location, which includes a nationally renowned owl sanctuary and collection.

Turn left and cross the main road, cresting the rise and walking down to the sharp left bend. Here go right along the bridlepath signed for Muncaster Fell via Fell Lane and commence the climb up this stony track. If it's clear, the views out to sea from this point extend across the Irish Sea to the distinctive profile of the Isle of Man. It's a long, steady haul for a good half mile before Fell Lane levels out for a while. Views to the right (south) open out occasionally through the woods to reveal the craggy heights of Birkby Fell and the distant upwelling of Black Combe. Passing into birchwoods, the rough lane reaches a fork. The way is ahead, but a short detour to the left brings you to the picturesque Muncaster Tarn, nestling in the woods, an ideal spot to recover breath before the next stage.

Walking ahead from the fork, in a short distance a waymark post is reached. Don't take the bridleway (right) but continue ahead, soon passing through a gate onto the grassy fell. Keep the woods to your left and rise gently with the track until the woods peel away to the left. Here you've a choice, either continue ahead along the grassy, narrowing track through the bracken or bear half-left to climb to the low summit of Hooker Crag, here picking up a path along the summit crags. Either way, you'll eventually end up at a gateway at the corner of a fell wall. If you choose the lower route, simply follow the well defined path, keeping left if in doubt and skirting the lower slopes of the crags to avoid the sometimes extremely boggy flushes of marsh. The views from this modest fell are remarkable, taking in the highest of England's mountains in the Scafell range and Bowfell, ahead, Pillar and the Ennerdale Fells to the north and the Coniston Fells to the south-east. Lesser fells proliferate, whilst ahead and left is the great green swathe of Mitredale Forest.

At one point you'll rise to a perched block of stone upon which is carved the legend "Ross's Camp 1883". Looking for all the world like one of the Neolithic cromlech monuments found in Pembrokeshire and

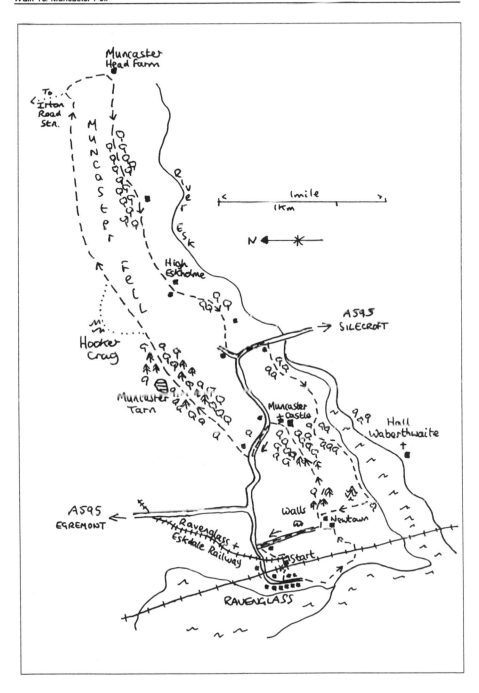

Cornwall, it is in fact a Victorian fancy, a picnic table used by a shooting party hosted by an individual called Ross.

Pass through the gateway in the corner beyond an unavoidable boggy flush and continue downhill, initially paralleling the wall but eventually parting company with this near to a scattered stand of small birch trees. The way all along this section can be difficult underfoot, both boggy and very tussocky, so take your time. Passing over a flat area of ground the path rises on an embanked route around a hillside before descending again through a gate and then through a growth of remarkably tall gorse bushes, eventually reaching a rough fieldside road near to a gate with a waymark post. The way here is right to Muncaster Head Farm. (If you wish to cut short the walk and return to Ravenglass on the narrow gauge railway then, instead, turn left and follow the bridleway which leads to Irton Road Station, about half a mile away).

Walk down to the edge of the farmyard here at Muncaster Head Farm. Take the walled track on the right and walk the few paces to the bridleway gate, once through which turn right, go through the right-hand gate and join the stony lane, split by a grassy spine. This is your route now for the next two miles, the initial fir woods giving way to mature mixed woodland with some fine specimen trees. Far ahead is an occasional glimpse of Muncaster Castle, your eventual target. Across the wide, lush valley of the River Esk the long horizon of fells has a foreground of two distinct crags, Raven Crag and Latter Barrow the product of localised volcanic activity aeons ago. In summer there should be a good number of butterflies along this wooded track, speckled woods and peacocks are particularly plentiful given favourable weather and food source conditions. Birds, too, are plentiful, including goldfinches and long tailed tits.

On reaching the buildings at High Eskholme the road improves to a tarred lane whilst the river meadows are manicured as a golf course. Pass by Yew Tree Cottage, resplendent with bright window boxes, planters and hanging baskets, roses and myriad assorted blooms throughout the summer, to the gate on the left about 200 yards beyond. Enter the golf course through this, walk ahead to the fairway and cross to a low bridleway post near the bunker. Look across to the woodland edge opposite where a further low waymarker directs you right, woods on your left, fairway to your right. As the fairway doglegs away look ahead-left for the gate into the woods. Another gate at the far end leads to a muddy path outside the woods, then a hedged track merging into a farm road. Turn right along this and follow it to the main road.

Reaching the road at a sharp bend, turn left and stay with it for about 200 yards to the old lodge house on the right. The Cumbria Coastal Way (CCW) Footpath is signposted along the driveway here, follow this through and out of the woods, continuing beyond across the foot of the landscaped parkland here immediately below Muncaster Castle. In about half a mile a waymark post confirms the way. Ford the brook soon after this and walk up to and through the gate into the woodland edge, then turn left. An ornate footbridge crosses the brook, then the path winds into the woodland, climbing high above the River Esk which loops in from the left. The woods here again contain many magnificent old trees, particularly large beech and chestnuts stand out. Rising to the wide forest track, turn left here with the CCW signpost to gradually lose the height just gained.

The path emerges onto a grassy promenade immediately above the river, a very pleasant section of the walk. On the opposite bank stand the lonely old farm and chapel at Hall Waberthwaite, these mark the far end of a long existing ford across the sand and mudbanks of the Esk. When you reach your end of the path leading down to the ford, marked by a noticeboard beside the path, remain with the path you've been following for another 150 yards to reach a fork. Here turn right, pass through the field gate and climb up to the high crosswall at the head of the pasture beyond the gorsey hollow. Go through the high gate-posted gate and bear half left, joining and tracing the line of wall around the foot of Newtown Knott. The dunes and winding channels of the complex estuary of the rivers Esk, Mite and Irt here present a picturesque foreground.

Two gates lead you into a rough lane beside the collection of barns and outbuildings at Newtown Farm. Follow this all the way to the junction with the tarred lane beneath the tall pine. Turn right to pass by the walls of the Roman Bath House, said to be amongst the tallest Roman remains still standing in Britain (Hadrian's Wall excepted, no doubt) and eventually the caravan and camp site on your right. At the end of the lane look for the footpath sign on your left for Ravenglass Station, returning to this and crossing the footbridge to find The Ratty Arms at the far side of the car park. The Ravenglass & Eskdale Railway, which provides a fascinating finale to the walk, was originally built to a 3 foot gauge, linking iron mines in the fells at Eskdale to the coastal railway where the ore was transhipped for use in the iron furnaces at Whitehaven, 15 miles to the north.

Walk 16. Irton Pike and the Irt Valley

Route: Santon Bridge – Irton Pike – Forest Bridge – Hollins Bridge

Terrain: One ferociously steep climb early on, then easy moor and farm roads

Distance: 6 miles

Start: The Bridge Inn, Santon Bridge. Ample parking.

Map: O.S. Outdoor Leisure sheet "The English Lakes, (SW)"

Access: The Bridge Inn is 3 miles SE of Gosforth (on the A595) along the road to Eskdale. Santon Bridge is also well signposted off the A595 both to the north and south of Holmrook. Alternatively, approach from Nether Wasdale, the village immediately below the foot of Wastwater.

The Bridge Inn (019467 26221)

In a marvellous setting beside the crystal-clear waters of the River Irt, The Bridge Inn is ideally situated for the discerning walker. The end of a spectacular undulating ridge which drops from Scafell Pike, England's highest peak, towers above the pub car park whilst the pleasant paths and "rides" of Mitredale Forest and National Trust-owned woodland are a short step away. Two hundred years ago this was simply a lonely pub and mail coach stop, today it's a comfortable country hotel, but one which retains the feel of a rural pub in its spacious bar. Part floor-boarded, part carpeted, the one large room is divided into a honeycomb of small drinking areas separated by recycled and reclaimed old beams and barn timbers. The bar itself, fronting a good sized open drinking area, is of unusual construction, resembling a clinker-built rowing boat. Replete with the standard range of country prints, old photographs, brasses and plates, the artefact collection also boasts one or two oddities including a cask-end from a barrel of the old State Brewery in Carlisle, closed in 1974.

One of the olden day characters of Wasdale was Will Ritson, erstwhile farmer, mountain guide and proclaimed "The World's Greatest Liar" in the 1880s. This title is still keenly fought for, the winner being elected each November; The Bridge is one of the locations for this unique championship. (Word is that politicians are not allowed to enter. Enough said.). Maybe it is that a good pint or two supped in front of a roaring log fire after a stroll in the fells gives the winner an edge. The beers upon which fanciful tales mature will include Jennings' Bitter, Cumberland Ale and Snecklifter, together with a guest beer selected at the whim of the licensee. There's plenty of time to practice your verbal deceit, as The Bridge is open 12noon -11pm (10.30pm Sundays) all year round. There's also a wide choice of bar meals available lunchtimes and evenings each day.

The wonders of Wasdale from Irton Pike

The Walk

The bridge celebrated in the pub's name is right alongside. Cross this and walk past the junction, heading for Eskdale and Broughton. Commence a steady climb and pass by the turn on the right, soon passing a Forestry Commission signboard for Irton Pike. On the left spruce and larch trees smother the slopes of Irton Pike whilst to the right the dominant roadside tree is a species of oak with a phenomenally large leaf, I'd hazard a guess at Turkey Oak. The road levels; ignore the footpath on the right for Plumgarth and continue to the lay-bys either side of the road about 150 yards further on. Pass through the gates of the lay-by on the left, immediately picking up a forest road that bends left within yards. You, however, need to go straight ahead into the trees. There follows a short but neck-craning climb, steeply up beneath the widely spaced trees and remarkably easy underfoot, a pleasant forest floor richly dressed with fallen larch needles and refreshingly clear of more than the odd fallen branch or tree.

The way is up, up and up; slightly favouring a left-hand course will allow you to strike a defined path, along which bear right to continue the uphill haul. You'll need many a rest stop, an ideal opportunity to attune to the wildlife in this airy plantation. Coal tit, goldcrests and even crossbills may flit amongst the higher branches; larger but more secretive are the red squirrels that still have a strong foothold in this Mitredale Forest and many other parts of Lakeland. Soaring above, the mewing call of buzzards is common, as is the laughing call of the yaffle (green woodpecker). Roe deer are also resident, and pine martens not unknown (though a sighting may best be reported at The Bridge in November...).

The path eventually breaks clear of the trees at a short scramble, emerging into a sea of heather and bilberries crowning the very top of this, Irton Pike. From this modest height are some of the most inspiring views in the Lake District. From the north and sweeping east, the rounded tops of Caw Fell and the mountains above Ennerdale sharpen to the peak of Pillar to culminate in the superb prospect up Wasdale, coming to its abrupt end at the graceful eminence of Great Gable. Lingmell, Scafell and Scafell Pike loom as the horizon loops south across the jumble of peaks from Bowfell and Crinkle Crags to the Coniston range and the long, undulating ridge of summits along Ulpha Fell, Corney Fell and the Combes. Due west the view is equally memorable, especially on a summers late afternoon with a declining sun silvering the sea, from which rises the wraith of the Isle of Man, its rounded summits of Snaefell, the Barrules and the central ridge around Slieau Ruy easily discernible. Nearer to hand, the green carpet of Mitredale Forest stretches away whilst the whole length of Muncaster Fell draws the eye to the immediate south. And, of course, there's Sellafield dominating the coastal strip.

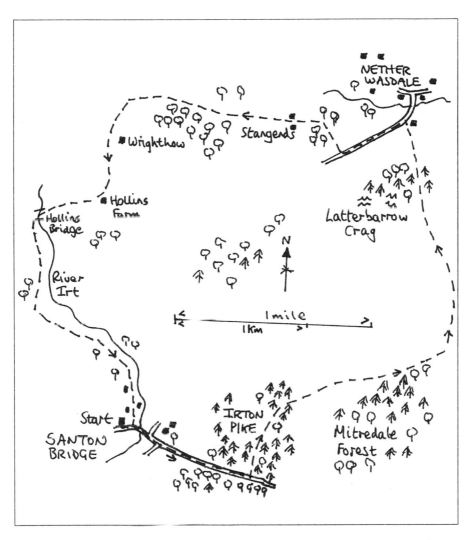

Tearing yourself away from these memorable vistas, descend along the path heading north-east – directly for distant Great Gable – and enter the firwoods along the wide path. This strikes through to a gap at the corner of two old walls, beyond which bear left with the path and remain with the firebreak to the step-stile over the fence at the woodland edge and the open moor of Irton Fell beyond. From here is your first sight of Wastwater and some of the famous screes that tumble from Illgill Head and Whin Rigg down to the eastern shore of England's deepest lake. Your target is the edge of the woodlands half-right and up the fellside, the uppermost plantations of Mitredale Forest. Plenty of sheep-paths and better defined tracks cross these heathery and tussock-grass covered uplands, simply drift towards the edge of the woods, joining a well-walked footpath which parallels the wall and continues to rise.

Stick with this path for nearly a mile, looking for the wide bridleway gate and stile in the woodland edge wall, not far from the top end of the woods. Don't go through this, quite the opposite in fact, turn left and join the obvious bridleway that cuts (sometimes very steeply, beware of hidden boulders and unyielding tussocks) down the northern flank of Irton Fell, falling all the way down to a woodland edge wall below the wooded crag of Latterbarrow. On reaching this wall turn right for the few paces needed to find the double gates leading to a stony path through these old pinewoods. Cross the plank footbridge and walk through to the junction of woodside paths, here going ahead towards Nether Wasdale. Within 100 yards bear right with the signpost and trace the woodland edge path, the last views up Wastwater a diversion to the right. Ford the shallow stream and pass by the diminutive tarn, heading across the pastures to the gate immediately to the left of the white-painted house.

The hamlet of Nether Wasdale, with its various hotel bars selling decent draught beers, is to the right across the bridge over the Irt. Unless you're particularly parched, however, turn left along the minor road and walk along the grassy verge for about 600 yards. Here on the right is a stony driveway signposted for Stangends. Join this, which soon curves left into magnificent beechwoods with some gigantic specimens towering a hundred feet and more. Pass straight through the farm complex, remaining on the hard-packed lane. The way is along this for the next mile and more, a pleasant walk along the edge of Foxbield Wood.

You'll eventually reach a point where another rough road comes in from the right. Here, bear left, soon passing the National Trust sign for Wrighthow Cottage near a cattle grid. Just before reaching the cottage itself, bear right along the gravelled road to reach a stile on the right beside a gate, just as the lane bends left. Over the stile, look across the pastures to the farm, then draw the eye to the left and somewhat nearer to you to sight a field gate within trees. Cross to this and then walk along the drive to the farmyard. Immediately before it climb the stile on the right, then the one on the left in just a few steps. Turn right inside the edge of the farmyard, continuing beyond along the tarred lane. This leads down to the remarkably humped Hollins Bridge, a design mirrored by the concrete utilities bridge immediately downstream. The Irt flows deep and clear here, look out for kingfishers and certainly for the plump sea trout swimming below.

Stay with the lane until reaching the sharp right bend and a sign declaring the road strictly a "farm access only" route. Turn right, then go through the gate immediately on the left. Head half-right across the field to gain the riverside path at the far end of the nearest strand of trees. From this point it is simply a matter of following the Irt downstream to return to the Bridge Inn, the final section being along a stony lane beside cottages and the old watermill, the leat for which comes off the Irt at a weir just downstream of the first cottage you reach.

Walk 17. Gurnal Dubs

Route: Burneside — Sprint Mill — Gurnal Dubs — Potter Tarn — Cowen Head

Terrain: One short steepish climb, fell road, field paths, back roads

Distance: 6½ miles

Start: The Jolly Anglers, Burneside.

Map: O.S. Outdoor Leisure sheet "The English Lakes, (SE)"

Access: Burneside is 2.5 miles NNW of Kendal and is signposted both from the town centre and the A591 road to Windermere. There is plenty of parking in the village and a car park adjoins the Spar supermarket on Hall Lane

Public transport: Burneside Station is on the Oxenholme to Windermere line and has regular daily trains from Lancaster, Preston and Manchester. (Turn right from the station drive to find the pub on the left in 400 yards). The village is also on the Kendal to Windermere (and beyond) bus route, with very regular daily services (service 555).

The Jolly Anglers (01539 732552)

The old building beside Burneside's main street dates from the 1660s and has functioned as a pub since the 1720s. An information board attached to the exterior of the pub details the chequered history of the premises and its connection with the Cropper Paper Mills, which industrial concern dominates the village. It lives up to its name, with a comprehensive collection of drawings of a variety of fishing flies, spinners and other lures dotting the walls. Old fishing rods clamped to some of the beams and a small side room all-but dedicated to the local fishing club, replete with photographs of local catches and champions, completes the main theme. Other decor includes some pencil sketches of wild animals – deer in particular – and odd items such as a couple of Tilley Lamps and a bakelite telephone.

The interior is basically one large room divided into distinct sections with the television and games part to the right as you enter. Warmed by a wood-burning stove in colder months, a varied complement of settles, upholstered benches and chairs leave lots of room to circulate in this friendly village local, an ideal place to rest and enjoy the Theakston's Best Bitter and a changing guest ale available at this Scottish & Newcastle tied house. At the time of writing the tenancy of the pub is changing hands. The opening hours (4pm-11pm) will undoubtedly be extended when the new licensees are in place.

The lonely fell road to Gurnal Dubs

The Walk

Turn left from the pub and left again down the rail-guarded roadway just a few paces along. At the end turn right to the main road and turn left along this, Hall Lane. Cross the bridge and walk on past the various factories of the James Cropper Paper Works and housing developments, soon picking up a separated footpath to the left of the road. Ignore the turn for the Dales Way and Bowston on your left and continue ahead to the end of the muddy footway. Off to your right is Burneside Old Hall, the shell of the medieval pele hall standing beside the slightly later farmhouse, the driveway still guarded by a gatehouse. At the sharp bend where the footpath ends at a junction, bear right with this surprisingly busy road and walk the 250 yards to the bridge over the River Sprint.

Turn left along the farm road your side of the bridge, signed as a path to Garnett Bridge Road. Follow this to the various buildings at the old Sprint Mill. Walk down to the yard just in front of the mill house and turn left, a low, home-made footpath sign directing you up a path between currant bushes and apple trees. At the end cross the course of the old mill leat, bear right and walk along the undulating path high above the river and the old leat – there are glimpses of fine falls, shoots and cascades down in the woods. You'll eventually leave the shelter of the trees as the river fades away to the east. Keeping the river well off to the right, follow the field boundary on your right and pass through the gateway, then a squeeze stile, the path then leading to a squeeze stile some yards in from the field corner. The next squeeze stile is visible in the far wall. Go through this, turn left the few paces to the field corner and climb the stone step stile. Face right and walk to the gates near the right hand corner but actually in the cross-wall. Once through the gates here pass by the oaks to your right and walk along the length of the long field to the gate at the corner at a road junction.

Go ahead here, pass by the buildings at Hill Farm and the telephone box. In less than 100 yards go left into the farmyard at Hill Fold, pass immediately to the left of the whitewashed cottage and follow the stony yard road for a further 30 paces to the gate. From here sight and walk to the field corner below the slate-built house and the whitewashed cottage beyond. Walk up the walled track to pass between these, joining the driveway beside the white cottage and passing by the miniature waterwheel at the garden edge. Look for the unusual concrete stile in the sharply angled field corner on your right just a few paces up the

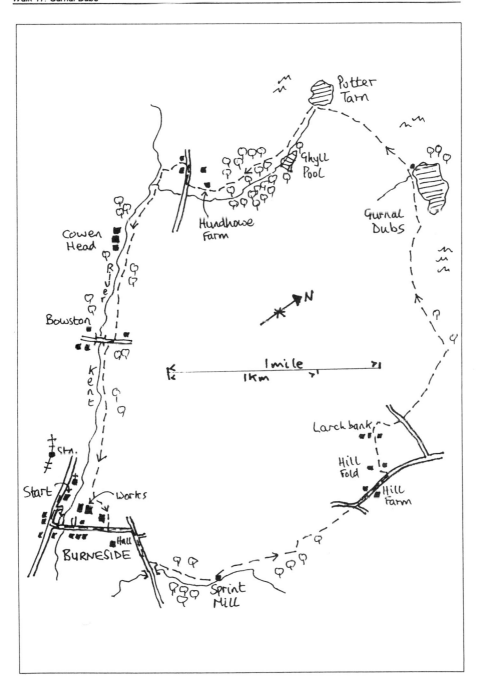

driveway. Walk diagonally up the field past the small outcrop to the gate in the top corner, leaping the brook en route. Beyond the gate at the top is a tarred lane. Cross straight over and go through the gateway opposite, there's a footpath sign here. Bear half-right to the wall on the far side and start the long, steady climb beside the wall, passing into the field beyond and rising to a gate onto a stony fell road at the head of the steepening grassy slope.

Turn left along this old road, but not before taking a few minutes to drink in the views to the east, for they'll soon disappear behind the near horizon. The distinct summit to the left is that of Whinfell Beacon, the long ridge taking the eye across to the pleasing convexities of the Howgill Fells, the highest of these remarkably unknown Pennine mountains being over 2200 feet above sea level.

Trace the fell road to Gurnal Dubs. This is a bridleway, the route is signposted to your left a short distance before the tarn, progress to the water itself being warned against by a peeling old signpost. The tarn looks natural, set in a sea of heather and small crags, more akin to a lochan in the far North-West Highlands of Scotland than a feature in the Lakeland fringes. Following the bridleway reveals that it's artificial, or at least partially so. It was created from two smaller tarns (hence the "Dubs" rather than "Dub") by the construction of a dam, the water being destined for the James Cropper factory in Burneside. The boathouse suggests that fishing may be practised here; a few minutes spent at the waterside should reveal many trout rises. The tarn also is home to grebe and mallard, whilst the surrounding heather moors are the ideal hunting ground for several species of raptor – sparrowhawk, peregrine and the elusive merlin amongst them. Listen, too, for the haunting call of the curlew.

Cross the dam and go up the wide green path to the stile. Climb this and the character of the immediate landscape changes, from heather moor to bracken hillside. Descend with the path to the dam of Potter Tarn in the middle distance. This was also created to satiate the thirst of the Cropper industry, as was the smaller reservoir lower down the valley. Tread the steps across the spillway, then turn left and follow the line of the beck, the path widening to a field road to pass above the smaller pond, Ghyll Pool, down to your left. At the wall bend left with the roadway, then swing right into the open oak woodland above the lively beck. Once through the gate keep right along the track, now high above the beck, gradually falling to a junction of routes and a selection of directional signs beneath an enormous sycamore. The way is right, through the narrow gate and down a walled sunken trackway, descending gradually to the old barn and outbuildings at Hundhowe Farm. Join the concreted driveway and continue down to the lane, turn right along this.

Just past the cottages in about 100 yards, a footpath sign points back-left through the farmyard. Trace a route below the high retaining wall of the garden on your left, at the gates turn right and follow the wide track down to the bridge over the River Kent. Don't cross this but turn left and, water to your right, follow the riverside path to the bank opposite the considerable complex of the former Cowen Head Mill, now largely redeveloped and extended as a development of luxury apartments. It's an inspired use of the old mill, but the finish is perhaps a little disappointing – white render in the main, with only a few finished in local slate.

Remain on the same bank and continue downstream, tracing a route between the golf course and the picturesque little gorge cut by the River Kent, then continuing across flat river meadows. Not far beyond the weir and ponded river at Bowston Mill, you'll reach a lane. Turn right, walk a few paces (don't cross the bridge) and take the path on the left, signed as the Dales Way. Follow this along the riverside through a number of pastures to the high, metal ladder stile over a brook. Beyond this the path continues to the edge of the new warehouse at Croppers Paper Mills. The fenced footpath traces a course around the edge of the complex, then a few extra steps to reach the footpath above the road. Turn right along this, then slip onto Hall Lane to return to the river bridge, the Spar shop and the main road. The Jolly Anglers is just a few paces to the right.

Walk 18. Heavenly Sites & Sights out West

Route: Gosforth – Calder Bridge – Calder Abbey – Scargreen

Terrain: Easy walking, several fords, one short & busy main road stretch

Distance: 7 miles

Start: Gosforth village car park

Map: O.S. Outdoor Leisure sheet "The English Lakes, (SW)"

Access: Gosforth is just off the main west coast road, the A595, about 6 miles south-east of Egremont

Public transport: The service 6 bus runs four times daily (except Sundays and Bank Holidays) between Whitehaven and Seascale via Gosforth. The nearest station (2.5 miles from Calder Bridge) is that at Seascale on the Cumbrian Coast Line.

Ye Olde Lion & Lamb (019467 25242)

For a village its size, Gosforth is very well pubbed. Rarely, however, will you find any of these drinking establishments featured in any guide-book or directory of drinking havens. Which is a great oversight, for all the pubs in the village offer a convivial welcome, decent beer and friendly faces at the start of (or the end of) a ramble in the local country-side. Ye Olde Lion & Lamb is a case in point. Set at the western end of the village's main street, it shares the road junction with two other pubs and the village post office. There's room outside on the cobbled fore-court for a few benches and tables, all-but shaded by the fine collection of hanging baskets, flower boxes and troughs; further fine weather out-door drinking is catered for by a beer garden to the back of the pub.

Photographs inside evidence the building's use as a hauliers base in Victorian times – the small bar to the right was the cart-house. The con-version to a pub probably dates from a century or so ago, ample time for the resident ghosts to stake their claim. The old cart-house is reputedly walked by the victim of a grisly stabbing whilst the form of a grey lady has materialised both in the main bar and in the upstairs of the pub - she's said to walk on the same day each month. Ghostly footsteps and trinkets disturbed from their place of display add to the fun, whilst one of the proprietors reports an unforgettable experience in one of the bedrooms early one morning (!).

The quality of the beer is first class, reflected in the award to the licensees of a Grand Master Cellarman award for consistency and excellence over many years. A free house, the regular beers are Theakston's Bitter, Jennings' Cumberland Ale and John Smith's Bitter, augmented by at least one guest offering usually from a smaller or micro-brewery. The main bar is a modest-sized L-shaped room with decorative beams, deep cot sash windows and a large tiled fireplace. An eclectic collection of old village photos, prints, paintings, brass and crockery fill nooks and crannies. There's also a serious accumulation of local sporting trophies, beatifically smiled upon by a signed photograph of the boxer Frank Bruno. The smaller room to the right is dedicated as a non-smoking bar and that to which those with children are funnelled.

A good selection of food is available, including curries, and discounted prices are granted to senior citizens. Food is served 12 noon-2pm and 6pm-9pm (hours are elastic, particularly in summer) whilst the pub itself is open all day every day (12 noon-11pm [10.30pm Sundays]).

The Walk

This walk includes an unavoidable section of main road with no verges to speak of. It can be quite busy as it's not far from the Sellafield complex.

The walk commences at the village car park, just 50 yards or so from Ye Olde Lion & Lamb (turn right from the pub's front door). Turn left from the car park and follow the main street the 200 yards or so to the junction for Wasdale, just past the village's garage. Some of the older buildings are passed by including the solid library building, originating in 1628. Stay on the Wasdale road to reach, on your left, a footpath signposted for Wind Hall. Turn up this (also the driveway to the Old Hall Hotel) but within a few paces divert into the churchyard on your right.

The modest church of St Mary dates, in its current guise, from about 1789 with later restoration. The foundation is centuries older, however, evidenced by the tall, slender cross near to the lych gate. This is perhaps the tallest, and certainly one of the finest, Nordic/Viking-Christian monuments in Britain. Controversy dogs all aspects of this 14-foot high cross, dates ascribed to it range from the seventh to the tenth centuries whilst the meaning and content of the copious carvings thereon are equally obscured by debate. The mix of pagan and Christian symbols appears to tell the story of the triumph of good over evil; the trunk of the cross is seen by some as the great ash tree Yggdrasil, foundation of all life to those Norsemen of old. Within the church are further fascinating artefacts from these times, including the massive "hogback" tombstones known as the Warriors Stone and the Saints Stone, the desecrated remains of other Norse/Christian crosses and the enigmatic "Fishing Cross". There's also a Chinese Bell captured at Anunghoy Fort during an escapade into Canton in the "Opium Wars" of the 1840s by one Captain Humphrey le Fleming Senhouse, member of a local family of worthies.

Return to the side gate of the churchyard and turn right up the driveway to and past the sturdy Old Hall, now a hotel. Dating from the 1500s the rendered front elevation disguises the solid, rough-dressed sandstone construction visible from the car park to the right of the Hall. Pass through the gate at the top of this car park, then the next gate a few paces further on. Keep to the left edge of this rough pasture and rise to the corner to pass through the gap in the wall just off this corner. From here sight the copse at the head of this large, rush-riven field and walk up to it, the way being potentially pretty boggy underfoot in places. Just in from the corner cross the little plank footbridge and the stile then climb the bank, heading for the top-left corner of the field beyond the trees.

At the corner are a number of gates, squeeze stiles and waymarks. Your route is ahead along the walled dirt road, rising slowly to the stand of pines at the hill's crest. From here the first views over to the nuclear complex at nearby Sellafield and the Irish Sea open out. Remain with the roadway to reach the buildings at Middle Boonwood Farm, the way getting muddier. The route is through the farmyard and out along the driveway leading from the farmhouse, shortly to reach a minor road. Cross straight over and continue along the gated dirt road opposite, once again in danger of being very muddy in parts. A diversion could be the great variety of wildflowers sprouting from the hedgerow and banked walls which line the route – foxgloves, knapweed, herb robert, gorse, broom, ragwort and elder brighten the way. Walking the route in September, a large flock of goldfinches was in evidence.

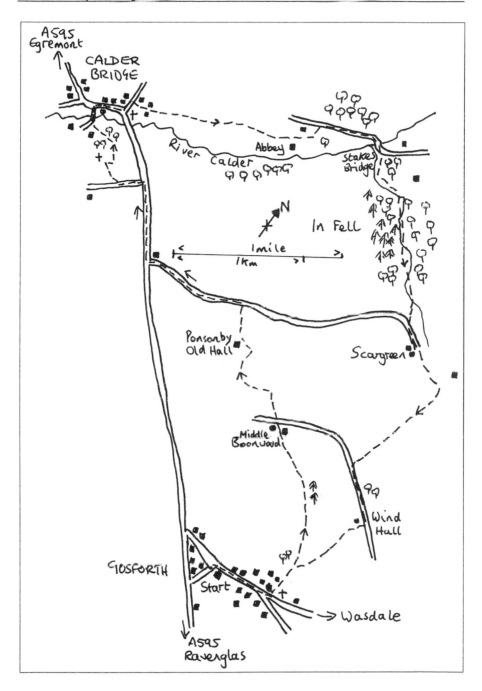

Dog-leg left with the roadway and walk on to and through the gate across the track *(N.B. not the one on the right)*, beyond which a long, narrow pasture develops. Follow this gradually right to the point where it merges into a large field immediately past a stand of gorse bushes around a pond. From here keep half-right to head for the right-most wooden electricity pylon visible towards the far corner of the field. Just beyond this fall to the footbridge across the brook and climb beyond to the stile in the corner of the plantation of Christmas trees. The path, at first somewhat indistinct and overgrown, traces a route between the trees and the boundary wall on your left to emerge at another footbridge and stile. Look left and head for the far corner of the small copse, ignoring the stile into these woods. At the far field corner turn left through the gate and walk alongside the barn here at Ponsonby Old Hall. Virtually opposite the far end of the barn is a stile set up to the right through a fence; climb this and trace the line of hedge on your left. The red-washed Old Hall Farm is all that remains of a complex of buildings originating in late Norman times, the hall was demolished many years ago.

Trace the hedge the one field's length to the far side. Gaps through this hedge allow views to the sea and several features of interest. Beyond the Sellafield complex may be visible the profile of the Isle of Man, about 40 miles out in the Irish Sea. Follow the horizon to the right from this and you may see further land. This is Burrow Head and "The Machers", the Wigtown Peninsula of Galloway in south-west Scotland, at about 50 miles distant usually no more than a smudge above a flat-calm sea. Much nearer to hand is the lump of St Bees Head beyond Egremont.

At the end of the field cross the stile and descend the awkward steps to the lane, turning down this to follow it to the main road about a half-mile distant. Turn right along this. It's a busy road and there are only limited verges. Fortunately the sight-lines are generally good and the stretch to follow isn't lengthy. It's common sense really, but face the traffic to the point opposite the "Slippery Road Surface" sign, here crossing to the "wrong" side to negotiate the bend, then cross back again. Not far round the corner is a lane on the left, just beyond the sign for Calder Bridge and signposted for Ponsonby Church. Go along here and in 150 yards or so turn right along the tarred drive to the church.

St Bridget's is built on what is essentially a raised platform on top of a low knoll, thus effectively surrounded by a deep, narrow "moat".

Technically it must be a Ha-Ha, built instead of a wall so as not to spoil the views from nearby Ponsonby Hall. Massive beech, oak and pine share the platform, the old Church House Farm stands between you and the looming towers of Sellafield. St Bridget's is essentially a Victorian pastiche on a medieval site; many of the memorial plaques within date from the late eighteenth and early nineteenth centuries whilst the oldest one seems to be a small brass plaque commemorating Frances Patryckson, daughter of "a Knyghte" and dated 1578. Nearly as venerable is the visitors book, with the first entry dated 25th July 1962.

Return to the little green gate across the "moat" and turn left and left again. Walk outside the moat to the corner with the fir trees, from here head half-right across the pasture to the open woodland just a stone's throw away. An obvious path (also serving as a horse-path) cuts a ledge across and down the steep slope within the trees to reach a waymarked stile perhaps 25 yards below the house. Trace the path through the undergrowth beyond this to emerge on a tarred drive near the entrance to Pelham House (the former Ponsonby Hall). Turn sharp right down this and follow it across the river to the main road here at Calder Bridge.

Turn right and stroll through the village to the old green on the left (long since tarred over) outside the early-Victorian church. Also fronting the green is The Golden Fleece pub. Walk along the lane for Ennerdale Bridge to the left of the church, ignore the footpath signposted through the corner of the churchyard, instead taking the path signed for "Stakes Bridge via Monk's Road" virtually adjoining. This passes beside the garage to end up in an open area between houses. Look for the narrow footpath from the right-hand corner (between a wall and Cupressus hedge) leading to a long pasture. Simply keep the wall on your left and walk east along the valley of the Calder, the river invisible to view, its course marked by the magnificent beech woods at the far side of the flat valley floor.

The mansion that has appropriated the location and some of the fabric of the old Calder Abbey soon comes into view. Remain alongside the wall and walk up to the wooden gate giving access to the manicured gardens of the old Abbey Farm, now redeveloped as private houses. Pass through the gate immediately on the left and walk alongside the rail fence to the stile at the far end of the gardens. Climb this and walk to and across the driveway, continuing ahead through the undergrowth to the metal rail fence. Turn left along the line of this and follow its somewhat overgrown course the short distance up to the lane. To your right, gaunt remains of the old Abbey draw the eye, the north aisle and transept still imposing in their ruin. The Abbey was a Cistercian foundation of 1134, well hidden from prying eyes in the heavily wooded valley (although the first build was burned to the ground by marauding Scots just months after completion); it was desecrated during the Dissolution of 1536. The mansion on the site appears to have Georgian origins. The site is not generally open to the public.

Turn right along the lane and stay with this peaceful byroad for about half-a-mile. The parkland on the right has some splendid specimen beech and oaks and some oddities. You'll soon see the skeletal trunk of an ancient tree, like a hollow oak gone several stages beyond. Look carefully and you'll see that it is in fact two trees, an ash and a field maple which have literally intertwined over centuries past, their trunks gradually rotting in parallel, although still very much alive. A little further along is a magnificent oak, its trunk and three or four of the main branches festooned with growths of fern.

Cross Stakes Bridge over the Calder, here parting company with the medieval Monk's Path you've been following as it climbs to an ancient packhorse bridge up in the fells, possibly the spot where the monks, jealous of their seclusion, traded in order to keep outsiders well away from the Abbey. In 50 yards or so go right at the footpath sign for Scargreen & River Calder. The gate leads to a short wooded path then the foot of a pasture. Once in the pasture bear half-left to walk beneath the stand of oaks, then remain outside the woods, following the lively Scargreen Beck uphill, water down to your right. Pass through the gate just above the Beck (and not the one through the hedge some yards above), immediately cross the sturdy footbridge and turn left, picking up a wide, green bridlepath which rises gently through the woods (initially above the Beck) along the flank of In Fell.

Two contrasting woodlands border this bridlepath. To the right the serried ranks of mature larch rise up the steepening fellside, just the sort of location to find fallow deer sheltering during the day; if they're there you'll hear them breaking twigs beneath their hooves long before you may catch a glimpse of one. To the left the open oak and birch woods is enlivened by stands of rowan, the bright red berries a delight in late summer. Buzzard, jays, various woodpeckers and a wide variety of smaller birds may catch your eye or ear. What will certainly take the eye are the rising folds of fells beyond these broadleaf woods, climbing steadily to the heights of Caw Fell and Lank Rigg, high above Ennerdale Water.

Your path rises much more gently. Near the end of the woods pass below and to the left of the field gate, following the path down to a ford, replete with suitable stepping stones. Follow the path the few paces beyond to the dirt road and turn right along this, dropping to recross the beck at another ford (no stones here), then climbing to reach a tarred lane. Bear left along this and rise with it to the farm buildings at the end, Scargreen. Just beyond the cottage the lane roughens and braids. You need to take the footpath signposted ahead through the gate just beside the small ash tree, leaving the bridlepath to fork left across another ford. You'll join the line of a stony field road alongside a wall (left) of large, rounded stones. Stick with this roadway as it bends right and rises to upper pastures. At the point where it gives out into a large field continue ahead, hedge on your

Gosforth's magnificent surviving Viking cross

left, to rise to a field gate. Go through this and continue up-field for about 100 yards to reach, on your left, a plank bridge and ladder stile. Cross these and turn right alongside the wall, tracing this to the very top of the field, climb the high stile here and turn right along the fell road.

Cresting its summit this fell road passes a stone boulder with the legend "Bleng Fell" inscribed. With no houses nearby it must refer to the modest heights to your left, merely the initial stirrings of the great mountainous waste known as Copeland Forest which towers above Wastwater. Ahead, splendid views open out to the south and east, from the coastal dunes and burrows at Silecroft up the great bulk of Black Combe and across the ridge of Corney Fell to the heights of Harter Fell and the Coniston group. Nearer to hand is the lower ridge of Muncaster Fell, backed by the higher line of Ulpha Fell. The rough road slowly descends to a junction with a minor road, turn left and follow this along the straight to Wind Hall Farm.

Just past the farm go right at the footpath sign, along the entry, through the gate, over the stile and along the narrow path. This ends at two closely spaced stiles, climb the first and turn left through the field gate – don't climb the second stile, beyond. Walk to the crest of the bank and Gosforth appears in the valley below. Also unfolding, off to the left, is an inspiring view up Wasdale to the awesome scree slopes which plunge from Illgill and Whin Rigg into Wastwater, itself not visible. Nearer to is the bald top of Irton Pike, its summit protruding through the firwoods of Mitredale Forest. This is one of those secret, unexpected views which makes exploring the Lakeland fringes such a pleasure.

Descend to the obvious path worn through the rushy pasture beyond the next fence and dropping towards the village. At the fence is a rusty, rail-fenced enclosure guarding a "Holy Well", doubtless centuries ago used as a place of baptism and, no doubt, said to have recuperative properties of its water. The well is still here, capped by a concrete cover and inspection hatch. Trace the path down the pasture to the gap in the wall, then head half-right to the wide gate at the foot of the field. You came through this at the start of the walk, simply walk down through the car park of the Old Hall Hotel and turn right to return to the main street in Gosforth, right again to find the car park and the village centre pubs.

Walk 19. Greystoke

Route: Greystoke – Red Barn – Townhead – Little Blencow

Terrain: Easy walking on back lanes and farm roads

Distance: 4 miles

Start: Greystoke Village Green. Parking at The Boot & Shoe, around the green or along the lane to the church

Map: O.S. Outdoor Leisure sheet "The English Lakes, (NE)"

Access: Greystoke is on the B5288 road about 4 miles west of Penrith.

The Pubs

This walk passes by two pubs, both very welcoming and worth a stop. Overlooking the village green in Greystoke is **The Boot & Shoe** (017684 83343), one of the "Pubmaster" chain of pubs. Originally a coaching inn, it's about 250 years old and has recently been extensively renovated and refitted to appeal both to passing trade (B&B is available) and the local community in this tiny village. Whilst the old beams and wood-panelled ceiling remain, the interior has been designed to reflect the current interior design fad for bare brick walls and quarry-tile flooring. The result is a comfortable mix of public bar & games room, a quieter lounge area and a separate dining room, also used as a drinking area and retaining some more traditional features. There's no particular theme to the decor or fittings, though there is a large collection of old biscuit and toffee tins and old mineral water bottles in the lounge area and more than a few mementoes of wartime days – air raid posters from the London tube and an old army uniform. Outside there are a few bench tables set on the courtyard. The beers may vary from month to month, with Boddington's Bitter the regular one and a changing beer from the "Tapster's Choice" range. Simple bar food and snacks are available at just about any time the pub is open (12 noon-11pm [10.30pm Sundays]), freshly made sandwiches, home made soup and the like.

Time your walk for a late summer afternoon start and you'll be able to pop in to **The Crown Inn at Little Blencow** (017684 83369); it's only open between 7pm and 11pm during the week, plus 12 noon-3pm at weekends. This hamlet only has a couple of dozen or so buildings, the Crown overlooks the triangular village green opposite the Methodist chapel. Licensed since at least 1723, the Crown offers Theakston's Bitter, Courage Directors and, as a free house, any of a wide range of guest beers, more often than not locally brewed. One bar serves the two main rooms, the smaller one to one side a games area, the other a long, low design, warmed by a wood-burning stove and with a noticeable equestrian theme; the walls are hung with halters, bits and assorted tacking ephemera, many photographs of racehorses, hunting nags and local equine personalities return your glance. There have been considerable improvements and modernisations over the past decade or so, but the Crown retains the cosy atmosphere of a small local inn, all too often lost when such buildings are renovated to cater for an ephemeral market style. In addition to the well kept beers a wide selection of meals are cooked to order during the evenings (7pm-9pm) and weekends (12 noon-2pm). It's an easy half-hour stroll back to Greystoke village green from The Crown.

The Walk

Cross the green to the post office and take the road which runs alongside it, leading to the village swimming pool and the church. Greystoke is largely an estate village, the old core dotted with solid sandstone cottages, houses and almshouses dating from mid to late Victorian times, some possibly the work of the eminent architect Anthony Salvin who worked on the remodelling of Greystoke Hall. The range of almshouses next to the post office have tiny colourful border-gardens in summer. Near to the swimming pool can be seen one of the old parish sanctuary stones, set at a distance from the churchyard and enclosing an area within which the Sanctuary of the Church could be claimed by fugitives (or those accused of a felony) in medieval times, in theory at least thus secure from retribution and punishment until their case could be presented and judged.

The church of St Andrew is a revelation. Many English village churches can spring a surprise, perhaps a Saxon font or medieval wall paintings; Greystoke's church is remarkable for its sheer size, out of all proportion to the village population of either today or in medieval times

The view to Mungrisdale Common from Red Barn

when it was founded. Remnants of this early period include a peal of four bells dating from the 1400s and the great east window, said to have been disassembled and secreted during the Commonwealth to hide it from Cromwell's fanatical puritans, only to be forgotten for 200 years, eventually being put back into position in 1848. The church is so large because it was developed as a collegiate foundation in the fourteenth century, a centre for training, instruction and missionary work. It also had six chantry chapels added to the nave where the local great and good could pray for the souls of the departed, and ensure that their benefaction would be remembered for centuries to come. Alabaster effigy tombs and brasses of generations of the Dacre family, the Barons and Lords Greystoke, evidence the long association of the principal family of this part of Cumbria with the college church. The light, airy church holds many points of interest and repays an extended visit.

The walk leaves the parking area in front of the church via the field gate between the churchyard wall and the row of cottages. Pass by the small stone building (the old hearse house) at the south end of the churchyard and walk on to a series of footbridges across brooks and drains sheltered by stands of oak and alder. Join the line of wood rail fencing, keeping this and the horse pasture to your left to reach a gate at the corner of a stable block, a part of the complex of training facilities here at Old Rectory Farm, base of a leading racehorse trainer. Go through the gate, turn left and trace the narrow path between the building and the firs to reach a footpath sign pointing across the fields to the right. This is not your route, however; you should, rather, continue ahead alongside the yard, crossing to the farm road at the next gate (step over the low fence as the gate will probably be locked) and tracing the track in your current direction, directly away from the stables to reach the swift flowing beck. There's a footbridge hidden beneath the low trees to your right, cross this and walk ahead the few paces to pick up the wide green lane, climbing gradually up this beneath the avenue of old ash trees to reach a surfaced road. Views to the west and south from the green lane include tantalising glimpses of the distinctive flat top of Blencathra rising beyond the long line of Souther Fell, to the heights of Matterdale and Threlkeld Commons and the dark peak of Helvellyn.

Turn left along the tarred lane and walk past Red Barn Farm, remaining with the ensuing surfaced, gated field road all the way to the main road about half a mile distant. Off to the right can be seen the distinctive architecture of Fort Putnam, one of a series of eccentric buildings built at the behest of Charles Howard, Eleventh Duke of Norfolk (owners of Greystoke) in the 1780s and named after battles, locations and heroes of the American Revolution which had occurred just a few years before.

On reaching the main B5288 turn right and walk along the verge to the entrance driveway to the Fort. Just a few yards beyond this cross the road and take the rough lane which passes below the garden of the lone cottage. Simply remain with this undulating byroad for the next mile and more. The modest increase in height has opened out better views west to Blencathra whilst ahead the long line of the North Pennines draws the eye, a horizon which includes Cross Fell, the highest point of the "Backbone of England". Just before the road bends sharply to the left you'll be able to pick out, off to the right, another of the odd buildings created for the Eleventh Duke, this one being Spire House or "Jefferson", built with a spire and tower apparently to irritate the tenant farmer, a religious devout who felt that churches and church architecture diverted attention form the true Word.

This byroad eventually forges a way between the farm buildings at Townhead to reach the scattering of houses and cottages at Great Blencow. Turn left and follow the quiet road around the bend and

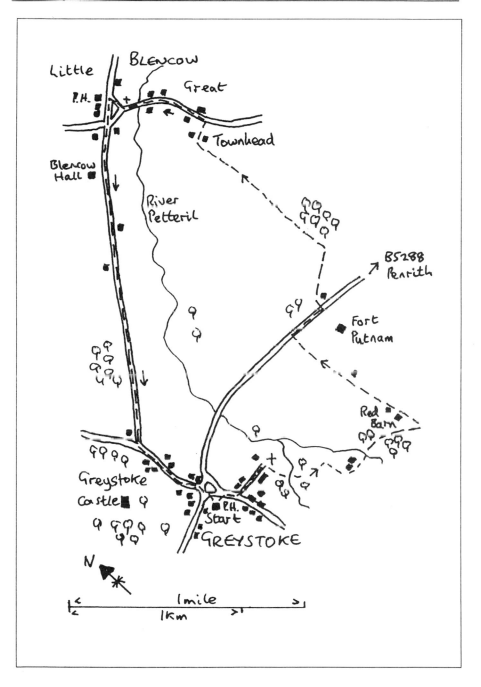

across the bridge over the little River Petteril. A few paces more and you'll reach the sloping village green at the heart of Little Blencow, which is, if anything, slightly bigger than Great Blencow. If you've timed it right then The Crown, standing above the green at the far side, should be available to wile away a few minutes within. With the Crown at your back turn right and take the Greystoke road from the green. This is the way right back to that village, a quiet lane which sees little traffic besides local and farm vehicles. In a few hundred yards on the right is the old Blencow Hall, a fascinating structure which is essentially two fourteenth century pele towers linked by a sixteenth century mansion built for one Henry Blencow. It's a private house, not open to the public but easily viewed from the road.

Just before the sharp bend and junction at the outskirts of Greystoke is the only reasonable glimpse you'll achieve of Greystoke Castle, an imposing Victorian work on a site originally built on by a Viking leader, Lyulph. It passed into the ownership of the Dacre family, major local landowners, then to the Dukes of Norfolk, the Howard family, to whom the castle and estates still belong. The park surrounding the castle is some five thousand acres, said to be the biggest private walled estate in England and, until recently developed woodland walks in the firwoods at the northern end of the park, it was the greatest expanse of land without public rights of way crossing it. During the Second War the park was given over to military training in the form of Polish tank regiment. The Castle remains a private home to which there is no public access.

Remain with the road as it passes between high stone walls to emerge at the village green, centred around the market cross. The market was granted a charter in 1350 but, like many others, the impetus that such a royal warrant was intended to give the village never took and the village remained just that. Off one flank of the green the main driveway to Greystoke Castle threads away whilst on another the Boot & Shoe awaits your custom beyond this wide grassy heart of Greystoke.

Walk 20. Bowscale and The Caldew Valley

Route: Hutton Roof – Mosedale – Bowscale Tarn – Low Mill

Terrain: Back lanes and field roads, one long, easy climb and descent

Distance: 7 miles

Start: The Horseshoe Inn, Hutton Roof

Map: O.S. Outdoor Leisure sheet "The English Lakes, (NE)"

Access: Hutton Roof is a scattering of houses and farms about 9 miles North-West of Penrith. Travel to Greystoke from Penrith along the B5288. In Greystoke take the minor road from the green signposted for Blencow and Johnby. In 400 yards keep left at the junction to travel to and through Johnby, continuing to the crossroads at Thanet Well. Turn left, pass by the caravan site then go straight over the crossroads in about one mile. The Horseshoe Inn is on the left in a further half a mile.

The Horseshoe Inn (017684 84354)

This is a long-established farmer's pub which has diversified into catering for the visitor market without losing any of that essential-yet-undefinable character which such isolated community pubs exude. Hutton Roof is no more than a couple of farms, an old school and the Horseshoe, set on top of a low ridge between the reedy lowlands of the Caldew Valley and the massive plantations of Greystoke Forest. This slight height advantage offers the chance of extraordinary views northwards from the grassy area next to the pub. Beyond the immediate pastures the low-lying plain of north Cumbria stretches to Carlisle and the Solway Firth, beyond which the hazy heights of the mountains of southern Scotland rise to well over two thousand feet above Moffat.

The whitewashed pub is at least 350 years old, originating as the smithy for the local farming community – the old derelict smithy outhouses were demolished a few years ago. The remaining parts of the building are deceptively capacious. The bar effectively splits the public room in two, the part you gain entry through is the games end, the quieter end to the rear retaining a splendid old blackened range still in daily use. The dining area completes the picture, diners coming from far and wide to enjoy and appreciate the first class food, all home prepared, which includes vegetarian options, curries, more exotic dishes and traditional English fare. As befits a pub of its ilk the decor is unfussy, much of it wood and plain wallpaper, the beams and shelves supporting the odd tankard or copper jug and a few old prints. The beauty of the Horseshoe is its unchanging, unhurried character. The local farming community keep a few sporting and games teams in the local leagues, accepting the B&B guests (5 letting rooms) as new locals as much as transient visitors, helping explain the high percentage of repeat visits by holidaymakers.

Behind the pub is a large lawn set with a few tables and benches, a very pleasant spot in which to idle away an early summers' evening. And evening it must be, because the Horseshoe is only open from 7pm-11pm (10.30pm Sundays). Time this walk well and you'll appreciate to the full the Jennings' mild and bitter, Cumberland Bitter and at least one guest ale; allow at least a very long 3 hours to work up a thirst, then sink back and drink in the tranquillity upon your return.

The Walk

Turning left from the pub, a gentle ascent past the few other buildings on the ridge-top crests the ridge. Immediately, fine views open out ahead across the flat expanse of the Caldew's marshy valley to the dramatic profile of the Caldbeck Fells, the very edge of the Lake District. The steep cliff of Scarth, directly ahead below the summit of Carrock Fell, holds the eye; to the north the gentler sweep of the lower fells each side of Carrock Beck ripple up from the plain whilst to the south the ever-rising flanks of Bowscale Fell, Souther Fell and the high plateau of Blencathra dominate.

Remain with the narrow road down the hill, turn left at the T-junction and walk for around 200 yards to the footpath signposted on the right. This grassy track commences a passage across the flat valley floor; apart form the odd old wall or fence this part of Lakeland's edge remains essentially uncultivated, the rushy, marshy land little altered since the last icesheet retreated about 15000 years ago. Reaching the old ford, now bridged, continue ahead along the winding track, the way

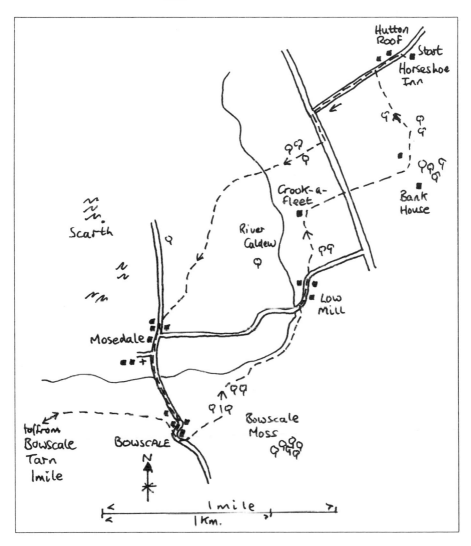

marked by the occasional thorn or wild cherry, soon giving out to the uninterrupted mosslands of Mosedale (to the right) and Bowscale (left) Mosses, coloured here and there by an eruption of foxglove. It's far from a deserted landscape however. Beside the sheep eking out a living from the tough grasses there are a good number of birds to look or listen out for, from the mewing call of buzzard wheeling overhead, the agility of kestrels hovering on the breeze (hence their alternative name –

Windhover), the distinctive croak of ravens and the squealing of jack-daws tumbling from their roosting and nesting sites on Scarth. Curlew, too, add their melancholy cry to be carried on the breeze.

Towards the far end of the moss the track becomes walled, eventu-ally emerging onto a minor road in the tiny settlement of Mosedale. Bear left and follow the lane past the imposing old yeoman's house, ignoring the gated road to the left in just a few yards. Whilst the way is straight along the "main" road, a short diversion up the lane on the right signed for Swineside brings you to the old Society of Friends (Quakers) Meet-ing House, the date on the door lintel of this low, barn-like building be-ing 1702, surely one of the oldest such buildings of this individualistic sect, albeit restored in the 1970s.

Back on the main road, cross either of the bridges across the River Caldew. The deep, shapely valley carved by the river is cut off by the distant rises of Coomb Height and Great Lingy Hill, the flanks of which echoed until a century or so ago with the sounds of miners toiling to win copper, lead and barytes, important in the then-new steel industry. Wind with the road up to the couple of farms and houses collectively known as Bowscale. As the road bends left past the final farm, look to the right for the signpost pointing the way along the wide bridleway for Bowscale Tarn. Here commences a long, gentle ascent around the northern flank of Bowscale Fell, a steeper final section bringing you to the deep, dark waters of the Tarn, hemmed in by the dramatic crags fall-ing directly from the summit of the 2303 foot peak.

The gloomy Tarn was a surprisingly popular destination for trippers in Victorian times, drawn here by the ancient legend of the immortal fish. These were (are...) said to be two schelley, a freshwater herring ma-rooned here (and in Ullswater and nowhere else) after the last ice age, living on the frugal pickings in this forbidding tarn and living on in leg-end. Wordsworth, who else, gave them a new lease of life and generated a minor tourist boom for this inaccessible, out of the way place, but fi-nally the Edwardians turned their gaze elsewhere and Bowscale Tarn has, ever since, been one of the quieter corners of Lakeland. Which means that it's usually quiet, peaceful and timelessly (if unfashionably) awe inspiring. Another legend was that at certain times and in certain light conditions, the reflection of the stars of the Milky Way was to be observed at the height of the day in the dark waters. All very Tolkienesque, maybe he picked up a few ideas from this legend when

Fellow walkers approach Mosedale

conjuring up Mirrormere, in the shadow of the Misty Mountains (in "The Lord of the Rings.").

Returning the same way from Bowscale Tarn, rejoin the minor road and walk ahead just a few yards, then fork left down along the stony road passing beside the old barns. This wide track strikes out along the edge of Bowscale Moss, the isolated birch wood way off to the right, backed by the crinkly limestone crags of Greystoke Park, a picture in its autumn hues. In perhaps 300 yards is a stone step stile beside a field gate on the left, just beneath the first tree of any stature along this mossland fringe. Take this stile, and the subsequent one along the field road. Cross a third stile and favour your left foot to gain the path along the embankment beside the River Caldew, remaining with this for about 700 yards downstream to the bridge and tarred lane. Leave the river here and go right, along the lane and through the complex of old buildings at Low Mill Farm, the mill now ruinous, an enormous old millstone propped against a wall a poignant reminder of better times.

As the road bends to the right look for the stile beside the gate on your left, once over which walk to the opposite right corner where there are a gate and slab bridge, closely followed by a footbridge and stile to tackle. Beyond these trace a path to and through the series of sheep pens, emerging in the farmyard at Crook-a-Fleet Farm. Join the drive-way and walk up to the minor road. Right opposite is a cattle-gridded driveway signed for Bank House Farm. Go up this as far as the sharp corner. Leave the drive here and aim half-left up the field, passing behind the ruined barn to an offset field corner. From here look up to the far top corner and climb the steep pasture towards this point, just a few yards below which is a stile. Pausing to recover breath gives time to enjoy for the last time the view to the south-west across to Blencathra and the great upwelling of fells to the east of Thirlmere, culminating in Helvellyn.

From the stile contour-walk to a further stile, continuing across the next rough pasture to a stone step stile down to a minor road. Turn right, climb the few paces to the top of the rise and look forward to finding the Horseshoe open just a further few hundred yards along the lane.

Walk 21. Back 'o Caldbeck Fell

Route: Hesket Newmarket – Nether Row – Howk – Caldbeck

Terrain: Gently undulating countryside, a few modest ascents

Distance: 5 miles

Start: Hesket Newmarket Green; village car park near The Old Crown Inn

Map: O.S. Outdoor Leisure sheet "The English Lakes, (NE)"

Access: Hesket Newmarket is signed off the B5305 Catterlen (just north of Penrith) to Wigton road and is about 12 miles north-west of Penrith. Alternatively, Caldbeck is on the B5299 road between Carlisle and Aspatria about 9 miles south of Carlisle.

The Pubs

This walk meanders between two of northern Cumbria's most delightful villages. Rather than choosing one over the other, I'll let you decide which to start from – there's a pub at each! Note that The Old Crown in Hesket Newmarket opens only during the evenings on weekdays, so time your walk accordingly.

The Old Crown, Hesket Newmarket (016974 78066)

Set at the foot of the long, narrow village green, this small, mid-terrace house has an engaging secret, this being the existence of its own brewery to the rear of the property. Here is brewed some of the finest beer you'll find in greater Lakeland, even the whole country. Named principally after some of the more prominent fells of the northern Lake District, strengths vary from the pleasant Skiddaw and Blencathra Bitters to the powerful Old Carrock Strong. Half a dozen or so regular beers are supplemented by occasional brews, whilst combining half-pints of the regular beers offers almost limitless scope for ensuring that no fell worth its name doesn't have a beer named in its favour! Taken together with the fact that the pub is a wonderful survival of a tiny old village inn of years gone by and you have a marriage made in heaven.

The pub's main room is also the social centre of the village, home to clubs, community notices and, for those with no time for chit-chat, racks of magazines and bookshelves crammed with paperbacks. There's barely room for the 5 hand-pumped bar, never mind the modest number of Britannia tables, wall benches and worn wooden chairs. The ceiling beams groan under the weight of countless pewter pots and pot tankards whilst an enormous yard of ale hangs above the bar. Wall space not taken with newsy notices is filled with CAMRA award certificates, old prints and deeds. To one side is an area given to pool and other pub games whilst a small dining area occupies the other downstairs room. Hours of opening are 5.30pm-11pm, with lunchtime opening for a couple of hours at weekends and occasional high summer days; food is served between 6pm and 8pm.

The Oddfellows Arms, Caldbeck (016974 78227)

A welcoming village centre pub with the advantage of all-day opening for much of the year, the Oddfellows is a Jennings pub stocking the full range of their beers (including specials such as the intriguingly-named Crossed Buttock....) plus a guest ale sourced from a wide range of the smaller breweries of Britain. Within the solid old building, the split-level pub caters for a wide variety of clientele, the upper levels' irregularly flagged floor well suited for muddy boots and housing a pool table and darts board. The bar, too, is split level, though the whole of the interior is essentially one capacious room, dotted with tables, wall benches and upholstered chairs in both the bar and lounge areas. Real fires are a feature in colder months. Aside from the usual ephemera of prints and photos there are a number of age-old posters of local interest (when did you last see a "Wanted, Pewet Eggs" poster?) and a small collection of giant fir cones in one window alcove. Outside are a few tables and chairs on a terrace beside the car park which essentially forms the core of the village's central area. A comprehensive selection of bar meals is available both at lunchtimes and during the early and mid evenings.

The Walk (from Hesket Newmarket)

The car park at Hesket Newmarket is to the left of the Old Crown as you look at it, on part of the old common land immediately next to Denton House Guest House at the eastern end of the village. Walk up alongside the long village green, passing the pub to your left. Towards the head of the green – commonly grazed by sheep – is the old market cross and buttermarket, next door to the former village bakehouse. The tiny township was granted a Market Charter in the early 1700s and added the suffix "Newmarket" to its original name. The sheepmarkets and fairs failed to take root, however, and the town never grew beyond the size of the original village. The top of the village, beyond the post office, is marked by a road junction and the remarkable Hesket Hall, built in 1630, an extraordinary mix of gables, wings and bays, odd windows and classical features. Its design is said to have a temporal interpretation (i.e. it's a giant sundial), or perhaps it was just a foible of the owner, Sir Wilfred Lawson.

The way out of Hesket Newmarket is along the minor road which runs in front of the Temperance Hall (on your left), signposted for Fellside and Branthwaite (also Uldale and Bassenthwaite). Perversely, the Temperance Hall has been identified as being once the village's brewery, serving perhaps a half-dozen pubs and beer houses. Ignore the left fork within yards and remain with the "main" minor road, rising very gently up a long slope to Street Head Farm on your left. Immediately beside (past) this turn left up the wide green path and walk up past the red barns. Go through the gate, walk a few paces to the stile on the right and climb this, then following this walled greenway to its far end with three gates and three stiles to choose from. Choose the middle stile (some yards up to the left of the middle gate) and head across the field to pass immediately beside the sharp walled corner, continuing beyond to the stile in the far field boundary Another section of walled old lane is joined here, remain with this to the crossing of roads at the far end.

Keep ahead, joining the roughening lane and passing by the small barn (apparently a camping barn). This pleasant lane contours the higher pastures marking the lower slopes of the Caldbeck Fells, the highest point up to the left being High Pike. In 1857 Charles Dickens and the novelist Wilkie Collins partook of a ramble up into the fells from Hesket Newmarket, assisted by one of the local publicans – maybe you're retracing their initial steps. Their ascent and mishaps are recorded in the short Dickens tale "The Lazy Tour of Two Lazy Apprentices". The curvaceous fell sides here are dotted with the remains of countless mining undertakings developed initially, perhaps, by the Romans in their pursuit of copper and lead. Few of the workings appear of any great size and many are invisible beneath grass and heather, although ones higher up in the fells were worked until very recently, principally for the mineral barytes, important as a flux in the steel industry. This fell road eventually meets a tarred lane just below the few cottages and farm at Nether Row. Above this hamlet are the most visible remains of levels and spoil heaps, still stark against the grassy fell sides.

Your way is to the right, remaining with this lane to gradually fall downhill to the outskirts of Caldbeck village. Beyond this rise the modest heights of Broad Moor, Faulds Brow and the other low, last upthrusts of Lakeland. At the foot of the lane go straight over the crossing road and follow the very narrow, part tarred part gravelled road down to the bridge across Gill Beck. Cross this and walk down to the little green.

At the road junction here is the village school and an isolated old building, currently a rare map shop but possibly once the village bakehouse. Bear left at this triangular green and trace the road along to the farm called Todcrofts on the right. Immediately past this, also on the right, go through the kissing gate beneath the pine tree and signed as a footpath to "The Howk". Keep towards the right-hand edge of the field to find a further kissing gate leading to a flight of steps descending to a footbridge. The Whelpo Beck has sheared down through countless layers of limestone to create a spectacular little gorge christened The Howk, up to 100 feet deep and clothed in ash, pine and sycamore. Upstream are foaming shoots, downstream enormous fallen blocks which perhaps move just once in a millennial flood. Behind, beside and above these blocks are a series of small caves, hollows and caverns cut by the erosive action of the beck which tumbles over falls and cataracts.

Remarkably, this natural paradise was partially tamed by Victorian engineers. Turn right off the footbridge and follow the narrow, potentially slippery path up to then down another flight of steps, the path suddenly emerging beside the towering remains of a water powered mill. This was a bobbin mill, built in 1859 and closed in 1908 and renowned for the size of its waterwheel, at 42 feet in diameter said to be amongst the largest in the country (but paling beside the 51 foot wheel of Parkend Furnaces in Gloucestershire and the famous Lady Isabella at Laxey, Isle of Man, all of 72 feet in diameter). This has long gone, but the sheer depth of the pit, the first remains you come to, give an idea of the vast diameter it must indeed have been. The gorge and partially restored and preserved works (the abandoned mill eventually burnt down in 1959) will detain you for a while, after which simply remain with the widening path, passing through several gates to emerge at a road junction at the edge of Caldbeck and a choice of route.

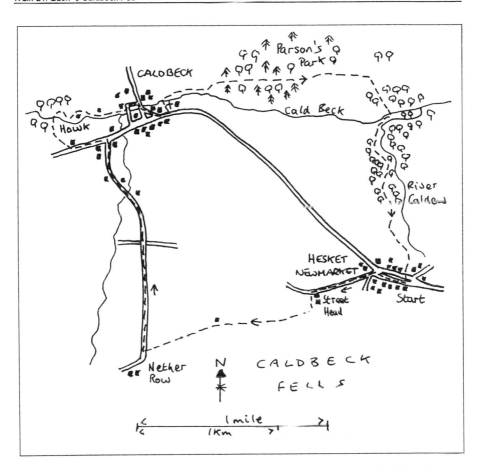

To the right the road leads over a bridge, passing several old mills (at its peak in the early 1800s there were as many as 13 mills processing cloth, corn, metals or bobbins) and the old village brewery (Caldbeck once had over a dozen inns and beerhouses serving a population far greater than that of today, up to 1800 or so in Georgian times). Turn left at the top to reach the Oddfellows Arms. Alternatively, carry straight on (and not left), pass by the old wooden village hall/institute and up to your left is the vast village green, complete with huge duckpond and collection of waterfowl. On the right just past the wooden building is the way down into the village car park. At the other end of this turn right, cross the bridge and climb the few yards up to the Oddfellows, on the left.

Whichever way you've come to the pub, from the front door walk directly across the car park and continue beyond the merging of the two roads, to reach the entrance to the churchyard on your left towards the end of the village. Caldbeck's St Kentigern's (or St Mungo's) Church stands above a low cliff above the Cald Beck. Kentigern's Well, immediately upstream of the packhorse bridge behind the church, is probably the original Holy Well, attracting first a basic chapel then a more solid structure named after this eighth century Bishop of Glasgow. Parts of the current church date back around 800 years, but its most renowned feature is to be found in the graveyard to the left of the main porch. Amongst a forest of sandstone tombstones a white one stands out, the memorial to John Peel, local huntsman immortalised in the well known refrain composed by his friend John Woodcock Graves. Also buried in this crowded churchyard is Mary Robinson, the celebrated "Maid of Buttermere". Next to the church is another of Caldbeck's many old mills. This one, Priest's Mill, retains a waterwheel perched high and dry above the beck and is now a centre for craft undertakings and a useful information centre for the surrounding area.

Cross the fine old packhorse bridge behind the church and turn right along the roughening lane. Pass through the gate across this track and remain with it to pass by the treatment works at the far end of the pasture. A gate beyond this leads into Parson's Park woodland, initially a gloomy larch plantation above the rushing Cald Beck. At the junction fork left with the bridleway sign and start a long, gradual rise up through the woods. At the next junction again follow the bridleway waymark (right), climbing now above the standing trees and levelling out along a ledge below a great felled area. Stay with this occasionally muddy forestry road, a couple of wind turbines soon appearing on a hillside in the middle distance, whilst off to the right (south) the long, rolling profile of the Caldbeck Fells comes into view.

Leave the woodland via the gate and continue ahead along the path into the long pasture for no more than 100 yards. Look down to your right to find the small stile (marked by a pole) over the fence – if you reach the line of dead trees on your left you've gone just too far into the pasture. Climb the stile and trace the narrow but fairly obvious path virtually straight downhill through the scrubby woods and then across a pasture to reach a footbridge over Cald Beck. This again is a delightful waterside setting, with a gorge downstream and, immediately ahead of you, the deep incised valley of the River Caldew which joins with the

Beck just below the gorge. Cross the footbridge and bear right, keeping to the left edge of the pasture to shortly find a gate leading into the trees.

This path gradually ascends through the edge of these ash and oak woods, eventually emerging into a pasture, across which a line of waymarker posts strings the way to the far end of the thorn-tree infested field. A further stretch of woodland path ensues, here and there very narrow and with a steep drop to the left down to the Caldew. Eventually the route leaves the woods, a pasture leading to a gravelly path, a foot-bridge and then a fieldside path. Aim for the kissing gate at the far side in line with the white cottage, which building is next to The Old Crown beyond the green here in Hesket Newmarket.

Hesket Newmarket's ribbon-like village green

Walk 22. Below The Gates of Ennerdale

Route: Ennerdale Bridge — Ennerdale Water — Howside — Bankend

Terrain: Easy back lanes and field paths, expect marshy sections

Distance: 5 miles

Start: Ennerdale Bridge village centre, parking at the hotel or around the green.

Map: O.S. Outdoor Leisure sheet "The English Lakes, (NW)"

Access: Ennerdale Bridge is signposted along minor roads off the A5086 Cockermouth to Egremont road. It's east of this road, about 5 miles north-east of Egremont and 12 miles south-west of Cockermouth.

The Shepherd's Arms (01946 861249)

An old coaching inn completed in 1704, this small friendly hotel faces the tiny village green at the centre of the compact village of Ennerdale Bridge. It's a popular spot with those ramblers in the know, for Ennerdale is one of the least visited parts of Lakeland; long-distance walkers on the Coast to Coast Path stop in but otherwise the area retains an air of tranquillity. The Shepherd's Bar is the place to head for, immediately to the right of the main part of the hotel. Within is a pleasant, light, unfussy, split-level room with a few wood panels, plain wallpaper and walls dotted with maps and prints. The licensee is a keen rambler so the whole feel of the place is very walker-friendly, right down to the daily weather forecast chalked on the board in the lower room off the bar and the selection of Wainwrights on one of the alcove shelves (and, one hopes, a copy of this book...). Walking boots and cagoules meld happily with the polished wooden floor, scattered with a few tables and wheelback chairs and warmed by the ubiquitous wood-burning stove. Comfortable couches dot the lower, carpeted "lounge" part of the bar area.

Open all permitted hours every day (well, maybe not all Christmas

Day...), the selection of beers is admirable. A free house, the regular house beers are Theakston's Bitter and Courage Directors, but it's the guest beers that take the eye, an ever changing panoply of delights sourced from far and wide. Of particular interest is the regular appearance of beers from Bushy's Isle of Man brewery, one of the few regular stockists of such beers on the mainland. Another plus is the excellent range of food and bar snacks, everything from soup to a wide range of vegetarian meals for which the Shepherd's has a good reputation. Food is available 12 noon-2.15pm and 6.30pm-9.15pm Mondays to Saturdays, all day on Sundays up until 9.15pm.

Fish farming in Ennerdale?

The Walk

There are probably more boggy stretches on this short walk than on any other in this book. Decent waterproof boots, or even wellingtons, are a must!

Opposite the Shepherd's is the village green, all-but filled in by the small village school. Keep to the left of this school and bear left at the junction, joining the narrow country lane signposted for Ennerdale Water. Simply remain with this for a good half-mile, the high fells of above-Ennerdale immediately making their presence felt close by to the right. The hedgerows here are particularly rich in climbing plants – honeysuckles, dog roses, convolvulus of various hues, woodbine and poison ivy lace the thorns, holly, low ash and oaks either side of the road. At the first junction, marked by a Forestry Commission board naming Broadmoor as the woodland, bear right and walk along past the cottages, continuing to the sharp left-bend in around 600 yards. Let the road bend away here, instead continuing ahead along the rough road to the farm at the end. This is an old mill; pass to the right of it and the remains of the mill, leat and associated works are revealed to the rear of the farm. Walk through to the high footbridge across the River Ehen, beyond which follow the muddy track to a gate, continuing beyond to the wide forestry road that runs along the foot of the steep lower slopes of Grike. Turn left along this road and walk with it to its end, Ennerdale Water now glimpsed ahead.

The forest road ends a short distance your side of a large, isolated house. Walk ahead along the grassy path to the gate into the back garden. Don't go through this but step up to the right to pick up a grassy path above the boundary wall, continuing then to and along the woodland edge path which eventually reaches the lakeside of beautiful Ennerdale Water. The way now is left to a wide bridge at the foot of the lake. (You could, if you've time and are so inclined, divert along the lakeside path for nearly a mile to the point where a crag virtually falls straight into the water. This is Angler's Crag, a renowned viewpoint up Ennerdale. Nearby once stood the much lamented Angler's Inn, demolished in the 1950s as a threat to the quality of the drinking water supplied from Ennerdale. A sad loss of a Lakeland institution known to have been frequented by Wordsworth and Southey).

Cross the bridge just below the low outfall weir and join the wide track which curves gradually along the foot of Ennerdale Water. This is essentially the dam along which you're walking, though it's hardly evident; only here and there are a few yards of old concrete visible, whilst the lie of the surrounding land confirms that this is a natural lake, increased in depth by only a few feet at most.

You'll pass through or by three gates in the next mile. Views all the while up the Lake are magnificent, the great forestry plantations of the 1930s on the northern shore and above the head of the lake hardly detracting at all from the scene. To the left (north) are the shapely fells of Great Borne and Starling Dodd, taking the eye to the bristly ridge of Red

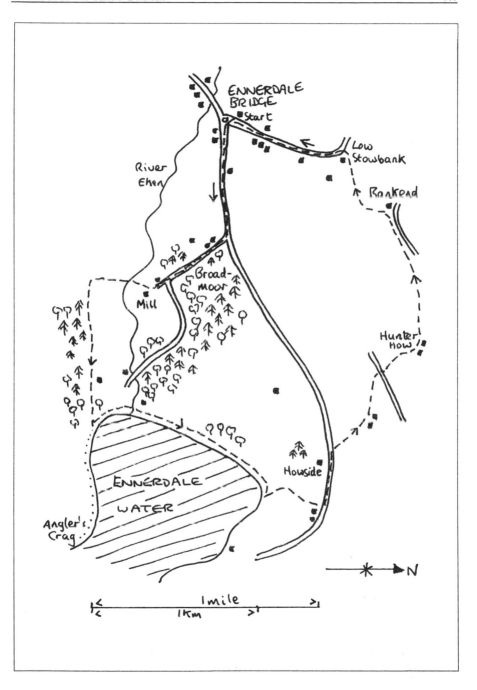

Pike and High Stile, separating Ennerdale from the far more popular Buttermere. Beyond the far end of the Lake rise the steep edifices of Pillar and Steeple whilst to the right are the lesser summits of Iron Crag, Whoap and Grike. Below the nearer slopes, Ennerdale Water spreads to its bulbous, wider foot; the craggy slopes of Bowness Knott (on the left) and Angler's Crag (right) can fittingly be described as The Gates of Ennerdale. It's a view difficult to surpass in the entire Lake District. So much scenery for so little effort, yet you may only see a handful of other walkers or visitors, so unfashionable is the place. Take time to linger and enjoy.

Some way past the second gate is an area of mature oaks and a line of age-old thorns, here also are some gnarled eucalyptus trees, the gum tree beloved of Australians everywhere. Pass through the third gate (it's the one where a length of wooden fencing stretches out into the water) and look immediately up to the left to sight and walk to a ladder stile. Climb this, step across the beck and turn right along its course, tracing it up through the tussocky pasture to the stone wall. At the far end of this is a plank footbridge and stile to cross, once over which keep the line of the old wall on your left and walk to the pale-green painted corrugated steel barn in the field corner. Go through the gate and turn left along the crumbling tarred road.

The narrow road rises gently between high hedges for about half a mile, gaps to the left offering final glimpses up the length of Ennerdale Water. The lane crests at Howside, the whitewashed old farm of that name sheltering beneath the pine covered crag on your left. Off to the right is a series of low, shapely fells collectively known as Loweswater Fell, a lonely area traversed by a few sheepwalks and pack horse trails.

Pass by the entrance to the farm yard (and ignore the immediate footpath to the right) and continue for around 100 yards to climb a stile by a footpath signpost on your right. There follows an extremely boggy field. Head slightly left to the line of the old hedge/wall. You need to trace this to its far end, the field to the left of it is perhaps slightly less of a quagmire. At the end is a wide wooden field gate this end of a low holly hedge. Pass through this and walk along the line of hedge on your right, cutting across the wider part at the foot of the field to find a stile in the open corner immediately below the tall, slender oak tree. Cross this stile, turn right and walk along the field edge. Let the hedge fade away to the right and walk ahead to the end of the field, aiming for the immediate left hand side of the stand of oaks. Here a stile drops down to a lane.

Virtually directly opposite, another footpath is signed as the route to High Stowbank. Climb the stile (beware the steep drop immediately beyond), cross the narrow footbridge and walk in the direction shown by the waymark arrow to pass by the isolated concrete fence-stay, looking ahead to the next stile beside a field gate.

Cross the slab-bridge and stile here, the banks of the little beck coloured mauve in summer by beds of fragrant water mint. Join the obvious field road and follow this across the pastures to the farm in the middle distance. Several gates/stiles take the route past the first cottage and barn and on to the side of the second cottage. Here on the left is a gate with a waymark arrow, pass through this and then climb the stile immediately on the right. You're in very rough, boggy pasture, the exit from which is at the far left corner where a short length of duckboard leads to two stiles. Continue through the rough tussocky pasture beyond the second stile to the right hand of two gates in the far corner, from where walk to the corner of the field near to the barn and farmhouse at Bankend.

Here there are two stiles and a veritable interchange of signposted footpaths. Climb the left-hand stile and turn left along the rough field road, a path signed for Low Stowbank. Go through the field gate at the end and turn right alongside the watercourse, walking to another stile and plank bridge. Once over these turn left and pick up the line of path tracing a ledge around the steep hillside, keeping well above the beck. Soon, the beck turns away at a right-angle. You should keep ahead here with the field path, aiming roughly towards the right-hand one of the two farms now visible. Climb the wooden stile at the dog-leg corner (with some very old stone steps just past it) and cross the thistley pasture beyond, straggly thorn hedge on your left, to another stile. Walk on to the far end of the long barn (ignore the first stile on the left just before the farm) to the stile, footpath signpost and steep drop down to the minor road. Turn left along the road to return the half-mile to Ennerdale Bridge.

Walk 23. Chapel Wood & Sale Fell

Route: Embleton – Wythop Mill – Chapel Wood – Routenbeck

Terrain: Easy back lanes, bridlepaths and woodland roads

Distance: 6 miles

Start: The Wheatsheaf, Embleton. Large car park to rear.

Map: O.S. Outdoor Leisure sheet "The English Lakes, (NW)"

Access: Embleton is on the old line of the A66 about 3 miles east of Cockermouth. Turnings to the village are signposted from the A66 by-pass. The pub is at the eastern end of the village.

Public transport: Embleton is served by regular daily (limited on Sundays) buses on the Workington–Cockermouth–Keswick–Penrith run.

The Wheatsheaf Inn (017687 76408)

The Wheatsheaf stands beside the narrow old A66 and below a series of sandstone quarries which have eaten into the long, low ridge linking the northern tip of Bassenthwaite Lake and the confluence of the rivers Cocker and Derwent where Cockermouth now stands. Around 250 years old, it's an old posting inn on the once busy old road between the coastal ports of west Cumberland and the inland markets of Keswick and beyond. A traditional and lively community pub, the full range of Jennings' beers are kept to perfection just a (long) stone's throw from the brewery in nearby Cockermouth. Within is a huge collection of brass artefacts and oddments, including post horns, plates, plaques, brass animals and suchlike which must be a real pain to keep buffed! The walls also hold some fine photographs of local beauty spots, copies of Edwardian posters extolling the beauties of Cumberland and an interesting old snap from 1895 showing skaters braving the frozen depths of Ennerdale Water.

The nice old wooden bar is the pivotal point of the pub, the main room curving round to three sides, the kitchen area to the fourth. Wall settles and a mix of old seats cuddle up to Britannia tables and the base tables of old sewing machines; the darts board nestles invitingly close to an open fire. Other pub games can be found in a separate games room upstairs. Outside are two large, peaceful beer gardens to the side and rear of the pub, both offering nice views across the low-lying pastures beside the complex system of becks and ditches to the woods and gorsey slopes of Sale Fell, Ling Fell and Embleton High Common.

Hours of business are 12 noon-2.30pm (ish...) and 6pm-11pm, with all day opening during high summer weekends. A good range of basic, high quality pub grub is available both lunchtimes and evenings until 9pm, look for the specials board next to the bar.

The Walk

This is a pleasant, easy walk at any time of year, but will be particularly delightful during the autumn, making the most of the fine woodlands encountered en-route, and also on a crisp winter's day with a hard frost and a dusting of snow on the higher fells.

Virtually opposite the Wheatsheaf a road drops between the village Post Office and the Derwent Lodge Hotel. Follow this down to the by-pass and cross straight over, picking up the narrow road winding gently up to the hamlet of Wythop Mill. The Mill is still here, a restored site generating income through accommodation and teas and having its fascinating machinery operational on many occasions during the year. It's an old water-powered wood-working mill; the old O.S. map on the wall inside the Wheatsheaf also shows a steam mill hereabouts. The modest, deep little millpond is held behind the wall on the west of the riverbank above the mill, easily visible from the far end of the old stone bridge. Adjacent is a fine row of old stone cottages bright beneath whitewash and blue sills, almost a Cumberland tradition.

At the bridge here is a crossroads. You should take the branch directly opposite that up which you walked into the hamlet, a narrow lane signed for Wythop Hall. Soon leaving behind the few buildings at Wythop, this peaceful lane traces a course up the vale between the Wythop Beck and mature woods up to the left, rich in old oak and tall Scots pines and dotted with the occasional wild cherry. At the fork just before the old Brumston Bridge keep left, rising to a gate across the road at the edge of the woods. This is the lane leading up to Kelswick Farm, simply remain with it and continue the long, steady climb into the low fells, gorse and heather-rich slopes rising steeply on your left over Dodd

Crag to the modest summit of Sale Fell, nearly 1200 feet high. On reaching the farm allow the driveway to sweep left into the yard whilst you continue ahead along the grassy track to the field gate (ignore the footpath to the right). Beyond the gate the green field road curves around the contour to reach the scant ruins of the old Wythop Church, just a few low walls at the woodland edge.

Immediately past these walls go through the vast, new (1998) wooden gate and ahead along the muddy bridleway into the woods. This very high stock fence surrounds the whole of these Chapel Woods, probably to keep out cattle and the secretive roe deer, which is still relatively common hereabouts; their fondness for baby trees would be a threat to the regeneration of these splendid woods. The woods themselves are a pure delight, a glorious survival of upland oakwoods, bright, light and pulsating with wild birds. In 600 yards or so keep left at the fork and continue to climb just within the woods. Looking up to the left reveals the results of centuries of pollarding, the oaks each having many trunks rather than a single one, a sure sign that they have been cut in past centuries to provide wood for charcoal burning, bobbin making and countless other uses. Another industry briefly flourished down in the valley of the Wythop Beck, visible through the trees as a wide, damp hollow of land secreted between these little known low fells. The manufacture of silica bricks early this century generated enough turnover to justify the laying of a railway to transport materials and finished products. The whole enterprise was short-lived, however, and has disappeared virtually without trace.

Eventually another massive gate provides egress from the woods, the wide bridlepath continuing the gradual climb around these lower slopes of Sale Fell. Off to the right (south) rise the higher slopes of Lord's Seat, Broom Fell and other rounded summits of these low hills to the west of hidden Bassenthwaite Lake. As the path rises, beautiful views unfold ahead to the sublime heights of Ullock Pike and mighty Skiddaw, the highest point of the northern Lake District. At one point the path cuts above a boggy stretch, near which point a line of thorns arcing away to the right from an old gateway marks the departure of the bridleway. You, however, remain with the path and climb easily upwards, a line of gnarled old thorns your companion for a short distance. This path is a dream – thick springy turf, hardly trodden with no sign of wear, a rare example of what many footpaths in the Lake District must have been like 50 years ago.

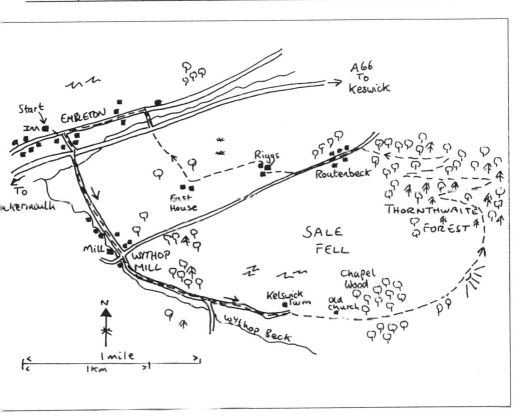

As the path levels out, views down to and along Bassenthwaite Lake are revealed to the right. Skiddaw still holds the attention to the east, below this near to the lakeside, the conical hill circled with a ruff of firs is Dodd. Given good visibility the views to the south and south-east seem to go on forever, across Keswick to the ridge of High Seat (between Thirlmere and Derwentwater) leading up to High Raise and beyond to the smooth curves of the Helvellyn massif.

For the next quarter mile or so the path very gradually swings north and undulates across this delightful upland common. More and more of Bassenthwaite itself comes into view, the scalloped bays of the eastern shore fringed with woodland and dotted with moored yachts. Beyond the most thickly wooded promontory, Bowness, you should be able to pick out the small church dedicated to St Bega, alone in the pastures within its circular churchyard. St Bega herself is an almost mythical figure, said to be an Irish Princess shipwrecked at St Bees Head in the Dark

Ages. Equally mythical, but in the heroic tradition, is Bedevere, Knight of The Round Table, whose starring role in Tennyson's "Idylls of the King" had him hurl Excalibur into a lake, to be caught in the grip of The Lady of The Lake. Tennyson's reworking of this ancient tale relies on inspiration gained whilst staying at Mirehouse, a mansion beside Bassenthwaite. The "Chapel nigh in the field..." of the poem was perhaps based on St Bega's, the "Great Water" over which the moon lay full, and into which Excalibur finally disappeared, was Bassenthwaite.

The path leads up to a gate into woodland. Cross into this and walk ahead to the hairpin bend within about 100 yards of entering the trees. Keep right here and commence a long, gentle descent along the grassy forest road through this northernmost part of Thornthwaite Forest. Initially the tress are predominantly firs, but soon a pleasant mixed forest develops, with fine stands of beech down to the right, Scots pines, oak and Sitka spruce to the left. It's just the sort of woodland in which to catch glimpses of red squirrels, roe deer and even an elusive pine marten (once in a blue moon....), whilst the trees echo to the high-pitched tweeting of goldcrest, Britain's second smallest bird, various members of the tit family and may still harbour the increasingly rare crossbill. It's also a prime location for goshawk.

After a while you'll come to a grassy path forking up to the left. Ignore this and continue along the wider forest road to reach the next hairpin bend. Curve round with this and continue downhill, starting a switchback descent through the woods. The next hairpin is to the left, go round with this and walk on to the next such tight bend. Here, don't go round the bend but, rather, continue ahead along the grassy path which branches off at the apex of the tight corner (if in doubt that you're at the correct corner, then just go round the hairpin for a few yards, where you'll find a low building on the left connected with waterworks). This wide grassy path passes by an exposure of slabby rocks on the left, and even starts to climb very slightly. Through the trees to the right can be glimpsed the very top of Bassenthwaite Lake, whilst up to the left the tall, mature larch all seem to have been blown over by a gale during their formative years, resulting in most unusual curved trunks.

In about a quarter of a mile a narrower path hairpins off to the right beneath a stand of enormous fir trees. Take this, falling down gradually to a short, steep scramble then a hairpin round to the left, the path also acting as a stream bed for a few yards. Remain with the path, keep right at the split and then bear left along the wider track to emerge on a minor road at the hamlet of Routenbeck. Walk ahead past the handful of large houses and isolated cottages which are the hamlet, continuing along the road for about a quarter of a mile to the driveway on the right, protected by a cattle grid, to The Riggs and Riggs Cottage. Trace this gravelled driveway down to the fold of houses, passing them to reach the old farm. Pass this too, winding behind the pebbledashed farmhouse and barn, over a decrepit gate and the few yards to another two gates, one ahead, one on the left. Go through the one on the left, picking up an old field road paralleling the hedge to your right (you're also following a line of electricity wires).

Passing through two further gates brings you to a rough farm lane leading past pens and a garden to a surfaced farm drive. Turn right along this. In the field to your right here, the smooth, mottled-barked tree with the spindly leaves is a modest sized eucalyptus. Stay with the rough drive to reach the main A66. Cross straight over, walk on across the weight-restricted bridge to the old road and turn left along this, following it back to nearby Embleton, and the chance to look at that old map on the wall of the pub which you somehow missed before setting out.

Walk 24. John Peel Country

Route: Ireby – Old Church – High Ireby – Ruthwaite – Uldale

Terrain: gently undulating countryside; back lanes and field paths; two long but gentle ascents

Distance: 5½ miles

Start: Ireby Old Market Place. Very limited parking here or at the Sun Inn.

Map: O.S. Outdoor Leisure sheet "The English Lakes, (NW)"

Access: Ireby is about 7 miles south of Wigton and is signposted off the A595 at several points (e.g. Bothel and Mealsgate). It is also signposted along minor roads from Castle Inn, (6 miles north of Keswick on the A591).

Public transport: The seasonal Caldbeck Rambler bus (Carlisle to Keswick) runs through Uldale on weekends from May to September and daily in late July to early September.

The Sun Inn (016973 71346)

This is one of the oldest pubs featured in this book, with documentary evidence of a pub on the site in 1586, a time when Ireby was far busier. The Robinson Bell family were publicans for many generations, an old photograph hung in the public bar recalls such earlier days. Another licensee was John Peel's grandfather, the family having many members in this and surrounding villages. The Sun has undoubtedly changed considerably since John Peel hung up his coat of grey in the bar here, but thankfully such changes don't include juke boxes or background muzak. Traditional pub games also retain a foothold (maybe that should be handhold) here, with shove ha'penny and table skittles still practised alongside the more common darts and cribbage.

Such entertainments perhaps pale in comparison to those enjoyed by the poet John Keats when he stayed at The Sun on his "Great Northern Tour" of 1818. Resting after a climb of Skiddaw, Keats happened upon a traditional country dance school where the participants

Ireby old church, lost in the fields

"...kickit & jumpit with mettle extraordinary, & whiskit & fleckit, & toe'd it & go'd it, & twirld it, & wheel'd it, & stampt it, & sweated it, tattooing the floor like mad". He even claimed that he enjoyed this more than the scenery, as it was patriotic! On occasion you may recognise a modern-day arts commentator and author of renown sharing the conviviality of The Sun with you; Lord Melvyn Bragg lives nearby and occasionally samples a jar or two of Cumbria's finest here.

Entering the pub through a short, gloomy passage the public bar opens off to the right, the slightly larger lounge through an arch to the left. The bar strikes you immediately, with its full complement of handpumps dispensing Jennings' entire range of Bitters – Best, Cumberland, Snecklifter and a changing occasional brew such as Cockerhoop or Crossed Buttock. To the right the room opens out to the great fireplace at the far end, dominated by a large wood-burning stove and high, wooden lintel. A collection of unusual settles is the main form of seating. A comprehensive mix of prints and brasses dot the walls, the great beams and cross-members decorated with a variety of oddments. A French window leads out to a peaceful garden with a few tables and chairs giving views across to the far fells. The lounge area is equally characterful, dotted with a variety of wooden tables, another vast and varied collection of ornaments and a model of a sailing ship taking up much of one windowsill.

Pub hours are 12 noon-3pm (not Tuesdays) and 6.30pm-11pm (7pm-10.30pm Sundays). Good home cooked food is available at all sessions except Mondays in winter (November to March).

The Walk

Signposting and waymarking of public footpaths around Ireby appears (in 1998) atrocious; only nearer to Uldale on this walk are such facilities in evidence. The initial half-mile out of Ireby is far from obvious and necessitates climbing several fences without stiles and one topped with barbed wire. The route is along a right of way, however, so persevere.

With your back to the Sun Inn turn left to reach the village centre crossroads in Ireby. This was once undoubtedly the market place; the market cross stands just up the road towards High Ireby. Granted a market charter in 1237 the village became an important centre for the local area, evidenced by the fine old Moot Hall which still dominates the west side of the square. As with many small market towns, however, its importance waned over the centuries and, despite a brief resurrection as a corn market 300 or so years ago, its fortunes failed and it became the quiet backwater we see today, a pleasant mix of old cottages and village farms, with only the occasional modern house in evidence. The Sun is the sole survivor of the village's five original pubs, although "Paddy's Bar" on the square, has added some additional interest to the local beer scene. The village church of 1847 stands at the north end of the village; within are far older artefacts and memorials transferred from the original church, strangely isolated from the village about 1.5 miles north-west and the initial target of this walk.

From the square take the road signposted for High Ireby and Whitrigg, climbing gently past the market cross and strand of cottages and farms to the outskirts of the village, all of 300 yards. As the road bends left you should go through the gate on the right and pass directly beside the farmhouse (seemingly abandoned, October 1998) with blue-painted sills. As with most paths hereabouts there's no footpath sign or waymarks, you should pass by the farmhouse to its right.

Pass through the next gate and head directly across the small pas-

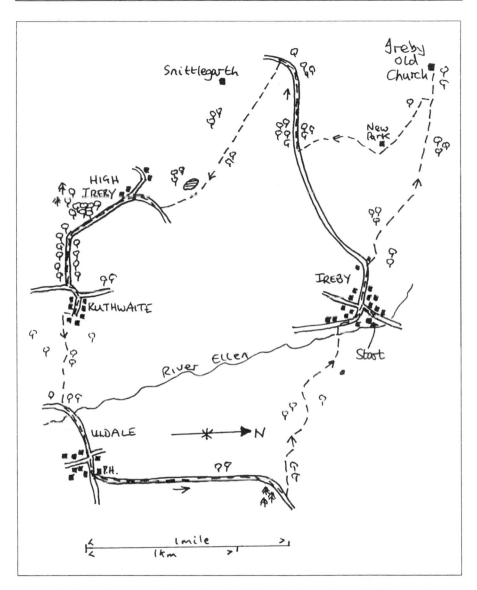

ture, looking for a small gap in the high hedge about half way down. Climb the rail fencing here and walk directly across the next field, again looking for a gap in the hedge. This one is fenced off and topped by barbed wire, here encased (when last walked) in a short length of blue plastic sleeving. Climb over here (it's immediately above a spring and section of rail fencing) and continue on the line straight across the field, looking for another gap in the line of hedge, this time with the benefit of a low stile. Head for about half-way down the hedge opposite where another stretch of fence, this time without stile and with barbed wire, has to be crossed, beyond which you're in a long, narrow field. Go straight across to the low stile, continuing beyond to the far fence roughly in line with the old church which is now visible in the shallow valley ahead. Cross another stile tempered with blue plastic sleeving and you're following the line of a grubbed-up old hedge to your right. Keep on heading for the old church, crossing several more stiles and a tarred lane before you reach the stone wall surrounding the graveyard of Ireby's old church.

The graveyard has some quite ornate and impressive gravestones; beside the sole slab-grave to the west of the church are the bases of two Norman (possibly earlier) crosses. Within, the church is simply an empty shell, devoid of almost all decoration and fittings. There are parts of one or two old crosses, a piscina and a few other artefacts. It is, in fact, the chancel of the 12th century church, the rest of it being demolished (from an apparently already fairly ruinous state) when the new church was built in Ireby. Strangely, it was not declared redundant until 1971 and the site is still consecrated. There's a useful little information board on the table at the east end of the room beneath the windows.

Leave the churchyard the same way you entered it and walk back to the tarred lane, turning right along this. In about a quarter of a mile pass by the buildings at New Park Farm on your right. Immediately past these go through the gate on the right (as ever, no waymarks or signposts), leading directly into a small enclosure crowded with ducks, chickens and other fowl. Bear left along the hedge and climb over the rickety fencing bordering this enclosure, then angle right to walk up the long pasture, heading for the copse of trees visible just beyond the slope top. Look for the point along the top fence where this dog-legs around the stump of an old tree. At this corner use the rickety old stile to cross the fence, then continue up towards the trees. A gate to the left of this row of ash trees leads onto a narrow road, along which turn right. You've gained enough height to open out views left to the long ridge of the Caldbeck Fells and the prominent heights of Skiddaw. If it's clear, then off to your right the mountains of southern Scotland take the eye, in particular Criffell (1866 feet), looming above the Solway Firth.

In a short distance the road starts a long, fairly steep descent into the valley of the delightfully-named Humble Jumble Gill. Stay with this quiet lane until you reach a narrow tarred lane on the left (about half a mile). Take this, your route for the next mile and more. It almost immediately starts to rise gently, a continuous climb for the next three-quarters of a mile. Off to the right across the fields is the many-chimnied old manor at Snittlegarth, whilst the obvious hill rising steeply from the surrounding pastures is Binsey, which stands about 3 miles to the north of Bassenthwaite Lake.

Cresting the top of the ridge, the lane levels out and a wide panorama is revealed ahead to Skiddaw, Great Cockup and the numerous other summits which go to make up the Uldale and Caldbeck Fells. A marshy pond takes the eye to the right, whilst beyond the first field on the left opposite this is the blind socket of an old lime-kiln, the small quarry that supplied it immediately behind. The limestone rock was roasted and crushed to a powder, then spread on acidic land (plentiful hereabouts) to improve its fertility. The crushed rock was also used as the basis for whitewashing and even as a patent medicine. Passing by sheep pens the lane joins a minor road. Bear right along this and walk through to the junction at High Ireby, here turning left opposite the old Grange Farm. A couple of farms and cottages are all there are at this remote hamlet.

A long estate wall separates the old parkland and estate woods from the lane. At one point there's an old drinking trough built into the wall, the inlet spout shaped like a writhing fish. The woods fade away to the right, from which point the lane is more of a stately drive lined with splendid old horse-chestnut trees. The junction at the end is at the hamlet of Ruthwaite. Turn left, then fork right within a few yards along the lane between the few cottages and farms here. In about 100 yards the lane peters out outside John Peels Cottage, said to be where the huntsman died of pneumonia (brought on by falling from a horse!) on November 13th 1854 aged 78. On your right here, and to the right of the whitewashed side of a cottage, is a footpath sign. Go through the gate, pass between the cottage and barn and climb the stile beyond into rough pasture. Keep the barns on your left to reach an old wooden stile by a tumbled wall. The stile has two waymark arrows, climb it and turn left down the line of the fence to another stile, once over which the land deteriorates into reedy, marshy pasture.

Follow the direction shown by the waymark arrow, essentially keeping the fence/wall to your right. In about 150 yards you should reach an offset gate and stile. Climb this and continue down into the shallow valley of the tiny River Ellen. Gradually angle away from the line of trees on your left to find the stub-end of a hedge beside a narrow ford. Step through this and look for the wooden footbridge about 100 yards ahead, once across which go through the right-hand of the two gates you'll shortly reach. An obvious path develops parallel to the wall, simply remain with this across further stiles to reach a minor road. Turn left and walk up to the crossroads at the foot of the green in the tiny village of Uldale.

The village features in the "Rogue Herries" series of novels by the popular Edwardian novelist (Sir) Hugh Walpole. Your way is straight ahead to the village pub, The Snooty Fox, a free house with a changing range of beers, now and then including Hesket Newmarket ales. Quality bar meals are also available lunchtimes and early evenings. Opposite the pub is a row of delightful old cottages wreathed in hollyhocks in high summer. Immediately beside the pub a narrow lane forks off to the left. This is your route, a potentially muddy old lane which rises gently but consistently for the next mile or so. Pleasant views across the shallow valley reveal Binsey and, beyond, some of the fells above Lorton Vale and Embleton. Skiddaw, too, remains as constant companion.

The lane eventually levels out, Ireby coming into view in the distance. Remain with the lane, by now split by a central spine of grass, to reach and pass three Scots pines on your right. About 200 yards beyond these a bridleway is signposted to the left. Take this, an initially grassy, then gravelled route between hedges, to reach the gate at the far end. Bear left along the farm road for about ten paces then go through the field gate set at an angle on the right. Head diagonally across this large field, aiming for Ireby. Climb the stile near the far corner and keep the thorn hedge on your right, walking beyond the end of the hedge to the second of two gates on your right. From this field corner gate aim to walk in line of sight immediately to the right of the two modern houses at the edge of the village. Cross a couple of stiles and walk ahead, the white-painted Ellen View cottage off to your right. You'll reach the river beside a bridge and a deep ford. Cross this bridge, walk to the minor road and turn right, climbing the steep bank to return to the centre of Ireby. The Sun Inn is to the right at the crossroads.

Walk 25. Blindbothel Parish

Route: Low Lorton – Stanger – Southwaite – Toddell Bridge – Cringley Hill

Terrain: Field paths, back lanes and fell roads

Distance: 7 miles

Start: The Wheatsheaf Inn, Low Lorton. Car park to rear.

Map: O.S. Outdoor Leisure sheet "The English Lakes, (NW)"

Access: Low Lorton is about 4 miles south-east of Cockermouth, on the B5289 road to Buttermere and the Honister Pass. It's also easy to reach from Keswick (c. 8 miles) via the B5292 over Whinlatter Pass, turning off in High Lorton.

The Wheatsheaf Inn (01900 85268)

In an enviable setting in the verdant Lorton Vale, The Wheatsheaf lies in the shadow of the majestic peaks of north-western Lakeland just 3 miles north of Crummock Water, one of the most scenic, yet under-rated, of the Lakes. The building itself is largely an old farm several centuries old, becoming a pub about 110 years ago. It's now the only surviving pub in the twin settlement of High & Low Lorton, the Horse-shoe having closed in the 1980s. This was a Jennings pub, as is the Wheatsheaf. This is most appropriate as it was at Swinside, just outside High Lorton, that the Jennings brothers started brewing on the family farm, moving to the current brewery site in Cockermouth in 1828. Memorials to the family can be found in the graveyard of Lorton church. The Wheatsheaf stocks four Jennings' bitters in summer, less during the quieter winter months.

Much of the interior of the pub is taken up by a popular (non-smoking) restaurant, doubling as a lounge bar outside of food hours (12 noon-2pm, 6pm-9pm every day), leaving just the cosy northern end of the long, low building as a convivial public bar, simply furnished with moquetted wall benches, the walls hung with many old black & white photos of scenes local and not-so. One feature you can't

miss is the vast collection of teddy bears on shelves, sills and other vantage points; the landlady is an avid collector, even the peaceful beer garden behind the pub has an ursine twist, being christened the Bear
Garden. It's a peaceful spot offering fine views up to the fells which
crowd this glacially-created pass between the jumbled heights of
Lakeland and the low country of the north Cumberland plain.

Opening hours are 12 noon-3pm and 6pm-11pm (10.30pm Sundays), but note that the Wheatsheaf is closed on Monday lunchtimes in
the winter months.

The Walk

*This walk is largely on surfaced roads. Don't let this thought put you
off as they are largely very quiet byroads or fell roads split by a spine of
grass, used more by sheep than vehicles.*

The River Cocker, which flows virtually past the Wheatsheaf's front
door, is the course of this walk for much of the first mile or so. To reach
its bank turn right from the entrance to the car park and follow the narrow road past the few cottages and houses that make up the top of Low
Lorton. Before reaching the right-hand bend just north of the village
look on the left for a footpath signpost, it's right opposite the roadside
village nameboard. Climb the stile and trace the little beck, soon reaching another stile. Cross this and head half-right across the long field,
aiming for another stile just to the left of the low, wide-spreading old
oak tree visible in the middle distance just beyond a metal rail fence.

It's well worth pausing at this stile and looking back to enjoy the
marvellous view beyond the Lortons. Crummock Water and neighbour-
ing Buttermere are invisible within the deep, glacial valley, but the
peaks which crowd these tranquil waters are conspicuous. On the right
(west) is the distinctive edifice of Mellbreak, towering above
Crummock Water, beyond which a ridge leaps ever-higher to Red Pike,
High Stile and Haystacks. To the east the great, graceful bulk of
Grassmoor is the terminal peak of an undulating ridge which includes
Grisedale Pike, Hobcarton, Hopegill Head, Ladyside Pike and White-
side. Off to your left the modest heights of Kirk Fell and Broom Fell, partially planted as part of the great Thornthwaite Forest, pale by
comparison to these giants.

Once past the stile look half left for another stile marked with a green
waymark arrow, designating a concessionary route through an environ-

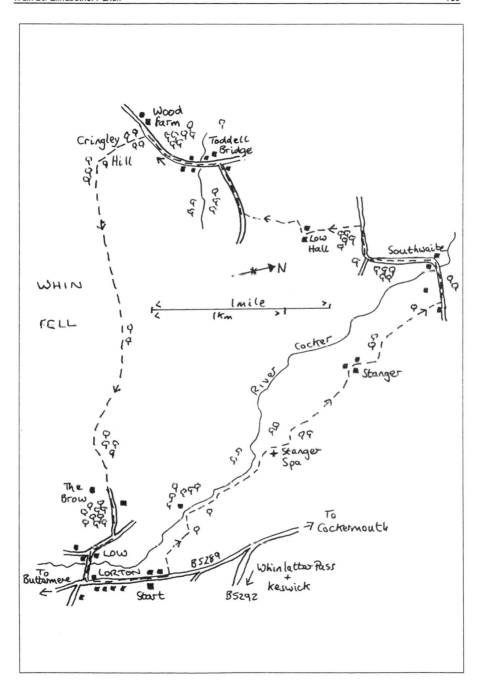

mentally sensitive area. This is the riverbank of the Cocker, which the path now follows for a considerable distance. The river flows cold and deep but is remarkably clear, fished by kingfishers and heron, much more visible than the timid otter known to live hereabouts. In spring and early summer this initial stretch of bank is ablaze with the vivid yellow flowers of the thick growth of gorse which borders the footpath.

A line of mostly waymarked riverside stiles is crossed before the route parts company with the river and reaches the small, roofless stone building at Stanger Spa, just beyond a stand of trees. In olden times this was a Holy Well, presumably so-designated as the waters were ascribed healing powers, a trait later exploited, to a small degree, during the spa boom of Georgian days. The well, now covered by a grid, is still there inside the building. Looking at the water today it's unlikely that anything but illness would result from taking the murky brown liquid! The site (and the nearby hamlet) may be named after the powerful Stanger family, the hereditary Foresters of the Derwent Fells from AD1437 to around AD1600, whose influence spread throughout the north-western part of today's Lake District.

Follow the obvious path from the spa across the reedy pasture, coloured in summer by great banks of meadowsweet. A stile beside the gate leads to a well-used path up the sloping field, soon joining the line of hedge on your right. Crest the top of the bank, go through the gate a few yards in-field (N.B. not the one on your right) and then keep the hedge on your right, following the track along to a gate at the narrow neck of the long field. You'll soon reach the range of buildings at Stanger. Pass by the renovated barn on your left and the farm on your right, immediately then looking for a blue bridleway arrow pointing right along a short, grassy track ending up beside an old cottage. Join the tarred lane here and walk uphill away from this cottage to find, on the left, a stile and footpath pole immediately below the line of electricity cables. Climb this and trace the edge of the field on your left to another stile, beyond which keep the line of trees and hedge close to your right. Step across the marshy beck and walk ahead along the sunken track, leading to a plank footbridge and a minor road. Turn left down this.

The lane crosses a narrow bridge over the River Cocker here at Southwaite Mill, long since converted to purely residential use. The low weir still partially impounds the river about 200 yards upstream, visible through the waterside trees. This is an excellent area to watch the antics of dippers as they search for larvae and other goodies on the bed of the swift flowing river. Stay with this occasionally busy back road for about half a mile; there's a wide grass verge, so the walking is easy. Keep right at the junction on the bend, heading for Eaglesfield. About 250 yards past the bend turn left down the tarred driveway for Low Hall, following it to the courtyard at this farm. Pass between the Hall, right, and the renovated barn, left, then turn right along the greensward to the gate at the far end of this long lawn. Pass through and turn left, then go through the gate beside the cattle trough. Ahead, the slopes of Whin Fell beckon. Skirt this large field along its left edge to reach a minor road, turning right along this. At the junction turn left and follow this quiet road past the imposing cottages and houses either side of Toddell Bridge.

In about half a mile you'll see the whitewashed Wood Farm on your right. Just before this, and on the left, a footpath sign points the way through a gate and up a dirt lane. A steady climb up the flank of Cringley Hill ensues, ending at a roughly surfaced fell road, known locally as Cringley Lane. Turn left along this and continue the now considerably less steep climb across the lower slopes of Whin Fell, wild and occasionally craggy sheep pasture at the heart of the scattered parish of Blindbothel. Whin Fell itself effectively cuts off views to the higher fells to the south until near the end of the walk. This is more than made up for by the views to the north and west, the mountains of Dumfriesshire rising beyond the Solway Firth to the north, the sea glinting in the sun to the west at Allonby Bay, north of Maryport. In the wide, low valley below you the town of Cockermouth stands at the confluence of the rivers Cocker and Derwent, about 3 miles away.

It's simply a matter of following this undulating fell road to its end, fine views up Lorton Vale to the peaks above Buttermere and Crummock Water unfolding as this old road starts to descend from its modest high point of just over 700 feet. Pass by the cattle-gridded entrance to "The Brow" and wind with the improving lane down to the junction. Turn right and walk along to and over the bridge across the Cocker, continuing to the main road. Turn left along this to return to the Wheatsheaf about 400 yards away, passing on your left the renovated pele tower at Lorton Hall. To your right across the fields is Lorton's St Cuthbert's Church, built in 1809 to replace it's medieval predecessor. It was in this original church that the famed Maid of Buttermere, Mary Robinson, married the bigamist John Hatfield in 1802, a cause célèbre in its day.

Lorton Vale from Cringley Lane

More Lakeland titles from Sigma Leisure:

BEST PUB WALKS IN THE LAKE DISTRICT

If you enjoyed the way that Neil Coates combines walking and traditional Lakeland pubs, be sure to get his companion book for complete coverage of the Lake District. This, the longest-established (and best-researched) pub walks book for the Lakes, is amazingly wide-ranging, with an emphasis on the quality of walks and the real ale rewards that follow! £6.95

WALKING THE LAKELAND FRINGES: SOUTH WEST

Continuing Sigma's exploration of the "fringes" of the Lake District, this guidebook by Mary Welsh is a celebration of the glorious countryside to be found in South West Lakeland. There's a total of 50 routes to choose from of varying difficulty and length (from 3 to 10 miles) ensuring comprehensive coverage of this beautiful area. Illustrated by Christine Isherwood, the well-known Lakeland artist. £6.95

A YEAR OF WALKS: THE LAKE DISTRICT

12 leisurely, circular walks - one for each month of the year - which visit exceptional locations in Cumbria. You have the option of a full or half day walk to each spot, whilst the month-by-month approach encourages you to walk in harmony with the changing moods of the seasons. Each route is enhanced by details of places to visit and notes on natural history, weather and landscape. Beautifully illustrated, including colour photographs. *£6.95*

TOWNS & VILLAGES OF BRITAIN: CUMBRIA

Ancient farms within patchwork fields of green and red, low South Lakeland fells and coastal views form the backdrop to this substantial account of the history and folklore of the towns and villages of Cumbria. Discover the Dacre Bears, corn mills, market towns, places of outstanding natural beauty, museums, railways, historic houses, churches and everything that is quintessentially Cumbria.   *£8.95*

NORTH LAKELAND WALKS WITH CHILDREN

Perfect for parents of reluctant young walkers – a collection of well-illustrated walks packed with interesting things to spot along the way. (This book was a prizewinner in the 1998 *Lakeland Book of the Year* awards. There is a companion volume for South Lakeland). *£6.95*

WALKS IN MYSTERIOUS SOUTH LAKELAND

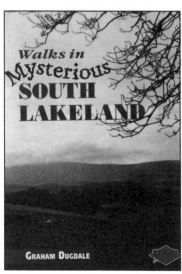

Old Nick, witches, wizards monsters, fairies, and grizzly monsters! Graham Dugdale intertwines intriguing tales of these dark beings with his 30 skillfully chosen gentle walks in south Cumbria. "This is a well-researched guide book, well written, with a welcome thread of humour." THE GREAT OUTDOORS. (Companion volume for North Lakeland also available.)   *£6.95*

All of our books are available from your local bookshop. In case of difficulty, or to obtain our complete catalogue, please contact: **Sigma Leisure, 1 South Oak Lane, Wilmslow, Cheshire SK9 6AR**
Phone: 01625-531035   Fax: 01625-536800   E-mail: info@sigmapress.co.uk
Web site: www.sigmapress.co.uk
ACCESS and VISA orders welcome.